ClearRevise®

AQA GCSE
English Literature

Illustrated revision and practice

An Inspector Calls
By J. B. Priestley

Published by
PG Online Limited
The Old Coach House
35 Main Road
Tolpuddle
Dorset
DT2 7EW
United Kingdom

sales@pgonline.co.uk
www.clearrevise.com
www.pgonline.co.uk
2023

PG ONLINE

PREFACE

Absolute clarity! That's the aim.

This is everything you need to ace the question on *An Inspector Calls* and beam with pride. The content is laid out in a beautifully illustrated format that is clear, approachable and as concise and simple as possible.

The checklist on the contents pages will help you keep track of what you have already worked through and what's left before the big day.

We have included worked exam-style questions with answers. There are also three exam-style questions at the end of the book. You can check your answers against those given on pages 59–60.

LEVELS OF LEARNING

Based on the degree to which you are able to truly understand a new topic, we recommend that you work in stages. Start by reading a short explanation of something, then try and recall what you've just read. This will have limited effect if you stop there but it aids the next stage. Question everything. Write down your own summary and then complete and mark a related exam-style question. Cover up the answers if necessary but learn from them once you've seen them. Lastly, teach someone else. Explain the topic in a way that they can understand. Have a go at the different practice questions – they offer an insight into how and where marks are awarded.

Design and artwork: Jessica Webb / PG Online Ltd

First edition 2022 10 9 8 7 6 5 4 3 2 1
A catalogue entry for this book is available from the British Library
ISBN: 978-1-910523-47-6
Copyright © PG Online 2023
All rights reserved
No part of this publication may be reproduced, stored in a retrieval system, or transmitted in any form or by any means without the prior written permission of the copyright owner.

Printed on FSC certified paper by Bell and Bain Ltd, Glasgow, UK.

THE SCIENCE OF REVISION

Illustrations and words

Research has shown that revising with words and pictures doubles the quality of responses by students.[1] This is known as 'dual-coding' because it provides two ways of fetching the information from our brain. The improvement in responses is particularly apparent in students when they are asked to apply their knowledge to different problems. Recall, application and judgement are all specifically and carefully assessed in public examination questions.

Retrieval of information

Retrieval practice encourages students to come up with answers to questions.[2] The closer the question is to one you might see in a real examination, the better. Also, the closer the environment in which a student revises is to the 'examination environment', the better. Students who had a test 2–7 days away did 30% better using retrieval practice than students who simply read, or repeatedly reread material. Students who were expected to teach the content to someone else after their revision period did better still.[3] What was found to be most interesting in other studies is that students using retrieval methods and testing for revision were also more resilient to the introduction of stress.[4]

Ebbinghaus' forgetting curve and spaced learning

Ebbinghaus' 140-year-old study examined the rate at which we forget things over time. The findings still hold true. However, the act of forgetting facts and techniques and relearning them is what cements them into the brain.[5] Spacing out revision is more effective than cramming – we know that, but students should also know that the space between revisiting material should vary depending on how far away the examination is. A cyclical approach is required. An examination 12 months away necessitates revisiting covered material about once a month. A test in 30 days should have topics revisited every 3 days – intervals of roughly a tenth of the time available.[6]

Summary

Students: the more tests and past questions you do, in an environment as close to examination conditions as possible, the better you are likely to perform on the day. If you prefer to listen to music while you revise, tunes without lyrics will be far less detrimental to your memory and retention. Silence is most effective.[5] If you choose to study with friends, choose carefully – effort is contagious.[7]

---

1. Mayer, R. E., & Anderson, R. B. (1991). Animations need narrations: An experimental test of dual-coding hypothesis. *Journal of Education Psychology*, (83)4, 484–490.
2. Roediger III, H. L., & Karpicke, J.D. (2006). Test-enhanced learning: Taking memory tests improves long-term retention. *Psychological Science*, 17(3), 249–255.
3. Nestojko, J., Bui, D., Kornell, N. & Bjork, E. (2014). Expecting to teach enhances learning and organisation of knowledge in free recall of text passages. *Memory and Cognition*, 42(7), 1038–1048.
4. Smith, A. M., Floerke, V. A., & Thomás, A. K. (2016) Retrieval practice protects memory against acute stress. *Science*, 354(6315), 1046–1048.
5. Perham, N., & Currie, H. (2014). Does listening to preferred music improve comprehension performance? *Applied Cognitive Psychology*, 28(2), 279–284.
6. Cepeda, N. J., Vul, E., Rohrer, D., Wixted, J. T. & Pashler, H. (2008). Spacing effects in learning a temporal ridgeline of optimal retention. *Psychological Science*, 19(11), 1095–1102.
7. Busch, B. & Watson, E. (2019), *The Science of Learning*, 1st ed. Routledge.

CONTENTS

Assessment objectives .... vi ☐

Context, language and structure

Priestley and *An Inspector Calls* .... 2 ☐
Context .... 4 ☐
Features of plays .... 10 ☐
Language techniques .... 12 ☐

Analysis of acts

Act One .... 14 ☐
Act Two .... 20 ☐
Act Three .... 24 ☐

Analysis of characters

Characters: Mr Birling .... 28 ☐
Characters: Mrs Birling .... 32 ☐
Characters: Sheila .... 35 ☐
Characters: Eric .... 38 ☐
Characters: Gerald .... 40 ☐
Characters: The Inspector .... 42 ☐
Characters: Eva/Daisy .... 45 ☐
Characters: Edna .... 46 ☐

Analysis of themes

Themes: Social responsibility .... 47 ☐
Themes: Gender .... 51 ☐
Themes: Generational differences .... 56 ☐

Examination practice **58**
Examination practice answers 59
Levels-based mark schemes for extended response questions 61
Index 62
Acknowledgments 64
Examination tips **65**

MARK ALLOCATIONS

All the questions in this book require extended responses. These answers should be marked as a whole in accordance with the levels of response guidance on **page 61**. The answers provided are examples only. There are many more points to make than there are marks available, so the answers are not exhaustive.

ASSESSMENT OBJECTIVES

In the exam, your answers will be marked against assessment objectives (AOs). It's important you understand which skills each AO tests.

AO1

- Show the ability to read, understand and respond to texts.
- Answers should maintain a critical style and develop an informed personal response.
- Use examples from the text, including quotes, to support and illustrate points.

AO2

- Analyse the language, form and structure used by a writer to create meanings and effects, using relevant subject terminology where appropriate.

AO3

- Show understanding of the relationships between texts and the contexts in which they were written.

AO4

- Use a range of vocabulary and sentence structures for clarity, purpose and effect, with accurate spelling and punctuation.

> The AOs on this page have been written in simple language. See the AQA website for the official wording.

PAPER 2
Modern texts and poetry

Information about Paper 2

Written exam: 2 hours 15 minutes (this includes the questions on poetry)

96 marks (30 marks for modern texts plus 4 marks for SPaG, 30 marks for the poetry anthology and 32 marks for unseen poetry)

60% of the qualification grade (20% for modern texts, 20% for the poetry anthology and 20% for unseen poetry)

This guide covers the section on modern texts.

Questions
One extended-writing question on a modern text (you will be given a choice of two questions, but you should only answer one), one extended writing question on the poetry anthology you have studied and two questions on the unseen poems.

PRIESTLEY AND *AN INSPECTOR CALLS*

An Inspector Calls is a play by J. B. Priestley which was first performed in 1945.

J. B. Priestley

J. B. Priestley (1894–1984) was an English novelist, playwright and broadcaster. Priestley served in the First World War (1914–1918), and his wartime experiences influenced his **socialist** views (see **page 6**).

> Socialists believe that individuals should share wealth evenly and that people should be treated fairly.

In later life, Priestley became more outspoken about **social responsibility**: the idea that everyone in society should look after those around them. Social responsibility and the unfairness of the class system are two overarching themes of *An Inspector Calls* (see **page 47**) which was written in 1944–5, just as the Second World War was ending (see **page 9**).

J. B. Priestley

An Inspector Calls

An Inspector Calls uses features of **detective thrillers** and **morality plays**.

Detective thrillers

Detective thrillers, sometimes called **whodunnits**, centre around a crime (usually a murder), where a detective conducts an investigation, and eventually reveals the culprit. In *An Inspector Calls*, the Birling family and Gerald are all suspected of being involved in the death of Eva/Daisy, but Priestley reverses the typical whodunnit narrative. Instead, the Inspector already knows that the family are responsible for Eva/Daisy's death, and the revelation is the family realising how their actions led to her suicide.

Comment: Each revelation increases the suspense for the audience, and builds to the final shocking revelation that Mrs Birling contributed to the death of her unborn grandchild.

An Inspector Calls continued

Morality plays

Morality plays were popular in the medieval period. They were religious plays used to convey teachings about good and evil. The characters in morality plays often had traits associated with the **seven deadly sins** (sins from Christian teachings): envy, lust, greed, wrath (anger), sloth (laziness), pride and gluttony (over-indulgence of food and drink).

Although *An Inspector Calls* is not a play about religion, Priestley uses the morality play format to teach the audience about the importance of social responsibility (see **page 47**). Priestley achieves this by using the characters to represent one or more of the seven deadly sins.

Character	Sin	Example
Birling	Greed	Birling's main concern is making money by pursuing *"lower costs and higher prices"*. He fires Eva/Daisy for asking for higher wages.
Mrs Birling	Pride	Mrs Birling refuses to help Eva/Daisy because Eva/Daisy pretends to be called *"Mrs Birling"*. She is offended that anyone from the working class would dare to use the Birling name.
Sheila	Envy, Wrath	Sheila was jealous that Eva/Daisy would have better suited the dress she liked. Sheila gets Eva/Daisy fired from Milwards *"just because I was angry and she was pretty."*
Eric	Gluttony, Lust	Eric has a drinking problem. He rapes Eva/Daisy when he's drunk.
Gerald	Lust	Gerald is unfaithful to Sheila and makes Eva/Daisy his mistress.

Morality in *An Inspector Calls*

Morals are a belief system which dictates an individual's understanding of what is right and wrong. Although they often overlap, morality is different to legality: just because someone behaves immorally, it doesn't necessarily mean they have broken the law. The Birlings and Gerald did not kill Eva/Daisy, however, the Inspector encourages the characters to decide whether their behaviour towards her was moral.

Sheila and Eric take responsibility for their actions

Comment: Priestley suggests that although the Birlings and Gerald are wealthy and privileged this doesn't make them 'good' or 'moral' people.

Some of the characters, such as Sheila and Eric, recognise that they have behaved immorally, whereas Birling and Mrs Birling, do not accept responsibility for their actions.

Comment: Eva/Daisy is one of the most moral characters in the play. For example, she turns down the stolen money. Despite her morality, she suffers the most because of her class.

Priestley encourages the audience to reflect on their own treatment and behaviour towards other people. He hoped that the play would inspire audience members to behave morally.

CONTEXT

The context of both the 1910s and the 1940s are important for understanding the deeper meaning of the play, and for demonstrating understanding of AO3.

Setting

An Inspector Calls takes place one evening in 1912. Setting the play in the past allows Priestley to create **dramatic irony**, as the characters comment on what might happen in the future. For example, Birling believes the passenger ship *The Titanic* is *"unsinkable"*, whereas the audience knows that *The Titanic* sank on her maiden voyage.

Comment: Birling's comments about *The Titanic* make him look foolish. If he's wrong about *The Titanic*, he could be wrong about other things too.

The play is set in England in a fictional city called Brumley, located in the north Midlands. It's described as being *"industrial"*, which implies that it has lots of factories, such as *"Birling and Company"* and *"Crofts Limited"*.

Comment: Poverty is often more pronounced in urban areas, so setting the play in a city allowed Priestley to highlight the inequality between the rich and poor more easily.

The Titanic sank in 1912

⭐ You need to comment on the play's context to get marks for AO3 (see **page vi**).

A wealthy British family in a horse-drawn carriage

Class

In Britain in the 1910s, families could be categorised into three social classes: upper, middle and working class. The class system was fixed, and it was difficult to move up the hierarchy. Upper-class families were the richest members of society and belonged to the aristocracy (families with inherited land and wealth). Upper-class families probably made up about 5% of the population. Middle-class families, like the Birlings, had money, but they earned it through running their own businesses. They accounted for approximately 15% of the population.

Comment: Birling is from the middle class, but he aspires to join the upper class. Gerald's mother, Lady Croft, is from the upper class, and Birling wants to impress her by telling her about the knighthood he is due to receive. For more on the character of Birling, see **pages 28–30**.

Class continued

The rest of society belonged to the working class. Working-class families were often poor, and needed to work for a living, usually in physical, unskilled jobs. Working-class livelihoods could be precarious. In the 1910s, employees didn't have any workplace rights or trade unions to support them, so they were often at the mercy of their bosses who could fire them without reason.

A group of working-class people from the 1910s

> Comment: Eva/Daisy is from the working class. Birling fires her when she organises a strike to try to secure higher wages, and she gets fired from Milwards after Sheila complains about her. Unlike today, there was no option to fight against unfair dismissal.

However, some members of the working class were beginning to speak out against poor conditions and unfair pay.

> Comment: In Act One, Birling comments that the *"miners came out on strike"*. This is a reference to an actual strike that happened in 1912, where one million British miners went on strike for 37 days, campaigning for minimum wage.

Some upper- and middle-class people were prejudiced towards the working class, viewing them as lazy and without morals.

> Comment: Priestley portrays Eva/Daisy as the opposite to this stereotype. She's hard-working and moral, rejecting the stolen money that Eric offers her. For more on the character of Eva/Daisy, see **pages 45–46**.

Upper- and middle-class people often believed that if a person was poor, then it was their own fault, rather than a symptom of an unfair society. There was little help for working-class people who were struggling. In the play, Eva/Daisy tries to get help from Mrs Birling's charity because there weren't any other options available to her.

> Comment: Priestley uses *An Inspector Calls* to demonstrate the unfairness of the class system. Eva/Daisy tries to improve her situation, but she keeps being pushed down by members of the upper and middle class. J. B. Priestley uses the play to try to encourage audiences to agree that more should be done to help poorer members of society.

Class continued

In 1910, the Liberal Party was in power in Britain. The Liberal government did little to intervene in people's lives. This suited the upper and middle classes because keeping the working class poor benefited the wealthy. Around the turn of the 19th century, political movements that campaigned for a fairer distribution of wealth and power, such as socialism, emerged. Socialism was unpopular amongst some of the upper and middle classes. Some people believed that the working class shouldn't rely on others for help, and it was their own responsibility to help themselves. However, some upper- and middle-class individuals rejected socialism because it threatened their position in society: if members of the working class had more money and rights, the upper and middle classes might have less power and money.

A political poster from 1910 suggesting that socialism threatened the prosperity of the country

> **Comment:** Birling calls socialists *"cranks"*. He sees socialism as a threat to his own wealth and social status.

Upper- and middle-class families did not mix with the working class. This meant that many upper- and middle-class people didn't understand the difficulties faced by the working class. Because upper- and middle-class people only socialised with each other, they existed in an echo chamber, where a person only encounters political beliefs which match their own.

Men and women were expected to marry within their social class. Even though upper- and middle-class families would socialise together, middle-class families would be aware that the upper classes were their social superiors, and would be expected to behave as such.

> **Comment:** There are hints that Gerald's aristocratic parents don't completely approve of their son's choice to marry a middle-class woman. Birling admits: *"your mother – Lady Croft… feels you might have done better for yourself socially."*

It would be unthinkable for working-class men and women to have a public relationship with someone from the upper or middle classes. Although romantic relationships between the working classes and the upper and middle classes probably did happen, they would have been kept behind closed doors.

> **Comment:** Both Gerald and Eric hide their relationship with Eva/Daisy to avoid a public scandal.

Gender

At the turn of the century, society was **patriarchal** meaning that women had a lot less power than men. Women were expected to be subservient, meek and polite.

> Comment: Etiquette (a code of politeness in society) was important to middle- and upper-class women. Mrs Birling attempts to uphold these rules. She frequently tells her family off for doing and saying things that are considered impolite.

Women in the workplace were paid less than men and all women, irrespective of their class, weren't allowed to vote. Women who tried to speak out against this inequality, such as the suffragettes who campaigned for votes for women, were often ridiculed and presented as undesirable. Society was often **misogynistic**: men were often prejudiced towards women, especially those women who did not conform to traditional values or society's expectations.

A misogynistic cartoon from 1910 deriding outspoken women

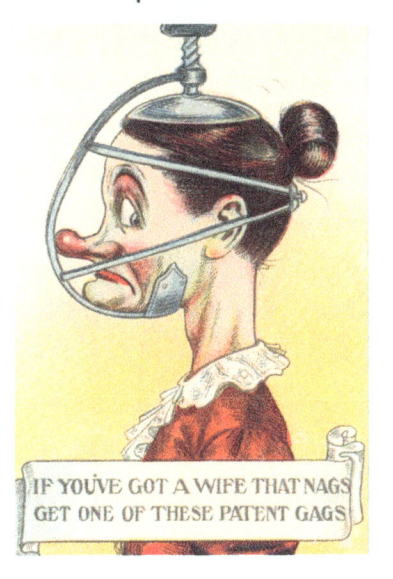

> Comment: Both Eva/Daisy and Sheila show signs of breaking away from female oppression. Eva/Daisy speaks out against unfair wages, and Sheila breaks off her engagement to Gerald and challenges her father: *"it frightens me the way you talk"*. For more on the theme of gender, see **pages 51–54**.

Expectations on women depended on their social class. Upper- and middle-class women, like Sheila, were not expected to work. They would be provided for by their fathers, and then by their husbands. Working-class women, like Eva/Daisy, needed to work to support themselves. Irrespective of a woman's social class, it was unthinkable to have a baby outside of marriage. Abortion was illegal, and there was little help for unmarried, single mothers.

> Comment: When Eva/Daisy is pregnant, she tries to get help from Mrs Birling's charity, but she is refused. With no employment prospects and no support, Eva/Daisy feels the only option available is to kill herself and her unborn child. Eva/Daisy is used to show the audience the need for government help for people who are struggling.

In the 1910s, there was often a double standard towards infidelity. Women were expected to stay faithful to their husbands, however, affairs committed by husbands were tolerated, provided they were discreet.

> Comment: When Sheila discovers that Gerald has been having an affair, Birling tries to explain Gerald's behaviour by saying: *"you must understand that a lot of young men—"*, implying that affairs were commonplace.

Gender continued

World Wars I and II contributed to changing attitudes towards women. Since a lot of working-age men were away fighting in the war, there was an increased demand for workers in Britain. As a result, more women entered the workforce, and had the opportunity to gain more independence. After the war, there were calls for women to have a more equal role in society.

Comment: Audiences watching the play in the 1940s would have recognised the progress that women had made towards equality since the 1910s.

Women working in a British Steel factory during World War I

World War I

The events of the play take place before the outbreak of the First World War in 1914. The First World War was a turning point for British society. Men from all classes fought alongside each other, and this highlighted the class differences at the time.

Comment: Many upper- and middle-class men were given 'officer class' positions overseeing regiments, whereas working-class men were often sent to fight on the frontline. Priestley was outraged that so many working-class men were sent to their deaths due to the incompetence and poor leadership of the officer class.

Following the war, politician David Lloyd George, wanted to make Britain a *"fit country for heroes"*. This meant improvements in employment as well as social conditions, such as housing and health. However, the promises made by politicians following the war didn't amount to much, which frustrated Priestley.

Comment: Priestley fought (and almost died) in the First World War. In the years following the war, he attended a regimental reunion where he learned that some of his fellow soldiers did not go because they couldn't afford suitable clothing. This angered Priestley. These men had sacrificed so much during the war, yet they were struggling to make ends meet. Priestley wanted to address this injustice.

Approximately 886,000 military personnel died during World War I

World War II

During World War II, Priestley broadcast a weekly series called *Postscripts* on the radio. The broadcasts were supposed to help improve morale in Britain, but Priestley also used them as a platform to argue for a better, fairer society after the war ended.

Postscripts was taken off the air after nine weeks. Partly because the Prime Minister, Winston Churchill, did not agree with Priestley's political views.

Comment: The play was written and first performed in 1945, just as the Second World War was ending and society's attitudes to social responsibility were beginning to change.

Following the end of World War II, the Labour Party, who had a lot of support amongst working-class voters, won a landslide victory. The British people wanted a government who would help the country to rebuild and recover following the war. The Labour government introduced the welfare state, expanded the National Insurance scheme and created the NHS.

The National Insurance scheme was first introduced in 1911, but it was expanded in 1948. Employers and employees pay a tax on earnings, and the money raised helps to pay for retirement, unemployment, disability and maternity benefits.

This was a turning point for government intervention in people's lives, and more support was available for the working class than ever before. However, these changes were met with resistance from some parts of society.

Comment: Priestley suggests that Eva/Daisy's fate might have been different if she had had access to government help.

The Labour government introduced the National Health Service (NHS) in 1948 despite objections from other political parties

In the exam, remember to include information about context to demonstrate your understanding of AO3 (see **page vi**).

FEATURES OF PLAYS

Plays are written to be performed, rather than read, so there are features in playscripts that are different to novels.

The information on **pages 10–14** will help you demonstrate your understanding of AO2. For more information on the AOs, turn to **page vi**.

Acts

There are three **acts** in *An Inspector Calls*, and the action is continuous: each act starts where the previous one ended. All the events happen on the same evening, in one room of the Birlings' house.

Comment: The continuous action as well as setting the play in one room makes the audience feel claustrophobic and trapped. This reflects how the Birlings cannot escape the Inspector.

An Inspector Calls takes place in one room in the Birlings' home

Structure

The play has a **cyclical structure**: it starts in a similar way to how it ends, with a police investigator on his way to interview the family about the suicide of a young girl.

Comment: This structure suggests that the Birlings are trapped in a loop, and the only way to escape is by accepting responsibility and changing their behaviour.

Priestley uses **cliff hangers** (moments of tension) at the end of all three acts. There is usually an **interval** between the acts, which allows the audience to take a short break to decrease the tension. Intervals would also give the audience time to reflect on the events and issues raised in the play.

Cliff hangers at the end of acts are also called **climatic curtains**.

Comment: J. B. Priestley wanted audiences to understand his message about the importance of social responsibility. He hoped that audiences would learn from the play and treat others with more compassion.

Priestley uses the characters' **entrances** and **exits** for dramatic effect. For example, at the end of Act One, the Inspector enters the stage just as Sheila tells Gerald that the Inspector already knows about Gerald's affair with Eva/Daisy. The Inspector's entrance creates a cliff hanger at the end of the act, and leaves the audience in suspense during the interval.

Naturalistic theatre

An Inspector Calls is an example of **naturalistic theatre**. This is a type of theatre which attempts to mimic real life as closely as possible. Priestley does this by writing realistic dialogue that sounds natural (see **page 12**), giving detailed stage directions to create a realistic set (**see below**), and writing the play as a piece of continuous action, with no jumps in time or scene changes.

Comment: Using naturalistic theatre techniques makes the play as realistic and believable as possible, so that audiences are more emotionally affected by the events of the play.

Stage directions

Stage directions are used to tell a director how the play should be performed and to guide the actors. Some stage directions tell actors when to enter or exit the stage or how to deliver a line, whereas other stage directions help to create a certain atmosphere or increase tension, for example, information about settings or sound effects.

Priestley includes very descriptive stage directions in *An Inspector Calls* which also give hints about the characters.

The dining room is of a fairly large suburban house... It has good solid furniture of the period. The general effect is substantial and heavily comfortable but not cosy and homelike.

Comment: The furniture helps to convey the Birlings' wealth, but *"not cosy and homelike"* hints at the discomfort and unease amongst the family.

Arthur Birling is... rather provincial in his speech.

Comment: *"provincial"* speech implies that Birling speaks with an accent and that his manners aren't refined. This tells the audience that he is not a member of the upper class.

The lighting should be pink and intimate until the Inspector arrives and then it should be brighter and harder.

Comment: The pink lighting could hint that the Birlings see things through rose-tinted glasses (i.e. a tendency to view past events in a positive, but often unrealistic, way). The change in lighting when the Inspector arrives implies that he will 'shine a light' on the behaviour of Gerald and the Birlings.

Inspector: *(cutting in, massively)*

Comment: The Inspector often interrupts the other characters. This shows his dominant personality, and how he isn't afraid to make others feel uncomfortable. For more on the character of the Inspector, turn to **pages 42–43**.

Birling: *(bitterly)* I understand a lot of things now I didn't understand before.

Comment: Stage directions indicate what tone of voice the actors should use when delivering lines. This can often imply a subtext: an actor's tone of voice can reveal more to the audience than the words being spoken. In this example, Birling's bitter tone indicates his hostility.

LANGUAGE TECHNIQUES

The dialogue in *An Inspector Calls* was written to closely match the patterns of natural speech. This contributes to the **naturalistic** style of the play.

Natural speech

Priestley tries to reflect natural speech patterns to make the dialogue as realistic as possible. He does this by using short (sometimes incomplete or single-word) sentences, **pauses**, **repetition**, **conversational language** and **interruptions**.

"Oh – I say – congratulations!"

Comment: *"Oh"* is often used in natural speech to show surprise, and this contributes to a conversational tone in the dialogue. The long dashes indicate pauses, which mimics everyday speech.

"Chump! I can't drink to this, can I?"

Comment: *"Chump"* is a slang word meaning 'idiot'. Using slang helps to make the dialogue sound less formal and more realistic. The tag question *"can I?"* is conversational, and more often found in natural speech.

"What – what did this girl look like?"

Comment: Repetition is often found in natural speech as a person thinks about what they want to say. Priestley uses it here to show Sheila's momentary shock.

"And if I could help her now, I would—"

Comment: Sheila's speech tails off, which is something that often happens in natural speech.

Gerald: *"Now listen, darling—"*
Sheila: *"No, that's no use."*

Comment: The long dash shows that Gerald's dialogue stops suddenly as Sheila interrupts. Interruptions are common when people are arguing.

12 ClearRevise

Allegory

An Inspector Calls is an **allegory**: it has a hidden, bigger meaning. The play isn't just about one family's experience, instead, the Birling family represent the whole privileged middle class, and Eva/Daisy represents the whole exploited working class.

> **Comment:** The name 'Eva Smith' sounds like Eve, the first woman in the Bible, and the surname, Smith, is one of the most common English surnames, which is derived from the job 'blacksmith', and relates to her working-class status. Therefore, Eva's name symbolises her role as a working-class everywoman (an ordinary or typical woman).

Allegorical texts often have a message that they are trying to impart. Priestley's message is that if the inequality of the class system isn't addressed, society will be punished (*"fire and blood and anguish"*).

Dramatic irony

Dramatic irony is a technique when the audience knows more than the characters. Priestley uses dramatic irony throughout the play, but especially in Birling's speech to the family at the start of Act One. For example, Birling predicts in 1940 Sheila and Gerald will be living in a world that will have forgotten *"all these silly little war scares"*. Audiences watching the play in 1945 would have just emerged from the Second World War, so this prediction would have made Birling seem foolish.

> **Comment:** Priestley presents Birling as foolish and unlikable because he represents those who are resistant to making society more equal.

Foreshadowing

Foreshadowing hints at something that will happen later in the play. It can be used to create tension or a sense of unease amongst the audience. For example, Sheila is suspicious of Gerald's disappearance the previous summer (*"except for all last summer, when you never came near me"*). This foreshadows Gerald's revelation later in the play that he was having an affair with Eva/Daisy.

> In the exam, remember to include the effect that these techniques have on the audience to demonstrate understanding of AO2 (see **page vi**).

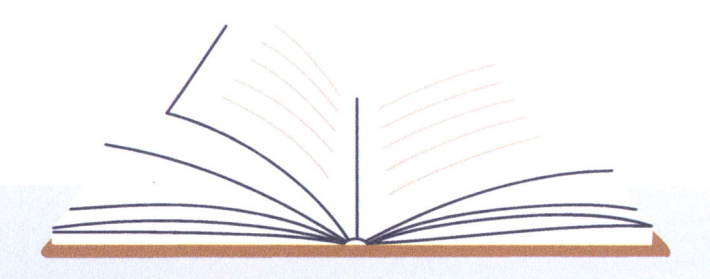

ACT ONE

Act One introduces the characters and the mysterious death of Eva Smith.

> **Act One**
>
> The Birling family — Mr Birling, Mrs Birling, their daughter, Sheila, and their son, Eric — are at home celebrating Sheila's engagement to Gerald Croft with a family dinner. The Birlings are a wealthy, middle-class family, and Mr Birling is a *"prosperous manufacturer"*.
>
> > **Comment:** The stage directions help directors to convey the Birlings' wealth to the audience. Their furniture is described as *"good"* and *"solid"*, there are *"champagne glasses"* on the table, and the men are dressed in *"tails and white tie"*. These details create the impression that the Birlings are an affluent, middle-class family.
>
> There are hints that Sheila and Gerald's relationship isn't quite right. Sheila implies that Gerald ignored her last summer.
>
> > **Comment:** This is an example of **foreshadowing**. The audience later discover that Gerald's absence was due to his affair with Eva/Daisy.
>
> Birling gives a speech to the couple. He's delighted by their engagement because Gerald's family run a successful business, and Birling hopes their companies can work together for *"lower costs and higher prices"*.
>
> > **Comment:** Even at his daughter's engagement party, Birling is preoccupied with how the marriage will benefit him. This presents Birling as selfish and greedy. See **pages 28–30** for more on the character of Birling.
>
> In his speech, Birling dismisses rumours about war: *"fiddlesticks! The Germans don't want war"*.
>
> > **Comment:** This is an example of **dramatic irony**. Audiences in 1945 would know that the First World War would begin just two years later in 1914. This makes Birling seem foolish, and suggests his judgement cannot be trusted. Since Birling represents **capitalism** and those who are uncompassionate towards the working classes, Priestley is keen to present him as a figure to be disliked and ridiculed.
>
> Birling often dismisses other people's views with words like *"fiddlesticks"*, *"rubbish"* and *"nonsense"*. He thinks that only his opinion matters, and anyone who believes otherwise is wrong. This suggests that Birling is small-minded, and he will not be receptive to other people's points of view.

Act One continued

After his speech, Sheila, Eric and Mrs Birling leave the room. Gerald and Birling discuss how Birling might be in line for a knighthood *"so long as we behave ourselves"*.

Comment: This is another example of **foreshadowing**. The rest of the play explores how Gerald and the Birling family have behaved improperly.

Eric enters, and Birling says that *"a man has to... look after himself and his own"*, ridiculing the idea that *"everybody has to look after everybody else"*.

Comment: **Social responsibility** (the idea that people should look after one another) is a central theme of the play. See **pages 47–49** for more.

Just as Birling tells Eric and Gerald that he doesn't believe in social responsibility, the doorbell rings. Edna, the Birlings' maid, announces that it is a police inspector.

Comment: The juxtaposition of Birling's line with the Inspector's arrival is deliberate. It suggests that the Inspector will challenge the Birlings' attitudes towards social responsibility.

The stage directions instruct the lighting to become *"brighter and harder"* when the Inspector arrives.

Comment: This lighting change reflects how the Inspector will make Gerald and the Birlings uncomfortable and will 'shine a light' on their behaviour.

Inspector Goole enters, and he tells Birling, Eric and Gerald that he's investigating the death of a young woman, Eva Smith, who died by suicide by drinking disinfectant.

Comment: The Inspector's visit is unexpected. He catches the family off-guard. He uses vivid, horrifying language to describe Eva's death: *"Burnt her inside out"*. This contrasts with the family's pleasant dinner at the start of the act, and hints that the Inspector will not shy away from making Gerald and the Birlings feel uncomfortable.

The Inspector's arrival changes the atmosphere of the play

Act One continued

The Inspector reveals that Eva, who went by several different names, had worked in one of Birling's factories. The Inspector shows Birling a photo of Eva Smith but doesn't let Gerald or Eric see it.

Comment: The Inspector uses the photograph to control the investigation. He only permits one person to see it at a time. This allows him to force confessions in an order that he wants. For more on the character of the Inspector, turn to **page 42–43**.

Birling describes Eva as *"lively"* and a *"good worker"*.

Comment: This presents Eva as a likable character, which generates sympathy from the audience. For more on the character of Eva/Daisy, see **pages 45–46**.

Birling admits that he fired Eva two years previously because she had helped organise a strike asking for higher wages.

Comment: Birling puts profit ahead of his workers. He represents the sin of greed. For more on morality plays and the seven deadly sins, turn to **page 3**.

Birling refused to increase his workers' pay, telling the Inspector: *"if they didn't like those rates, they could go and work somewhere else."*

Comment: Eric seems more sympathetic towards the strikers than his father: *"Why shouldn't they try for higher wages?"*. This hints that the younger generation might be more receptive to the Inspector's message and more tolerant to social responsibility than the older Birlings. For more on the theme of generational differences, turn to **pages 56–57**.

The Inspector remarks about the strikes: *"it's better to ask for the earth, than to take it"*.

Comment: From the outset, it's clear that the Inspector isn't impartial in the investigation, and that he's prepared to confront the Birling family's attitudes to class inequality. J. B. Priestley uses the Inspector as a mouthpiece to voice his own opinions on social responsibility.

When Birling realises that the Inspector is prepared to stand up to him, Birling reminds the Inspector that he knows the Chief Constable of the local police force.

Comment: Birling thinks he can use his power and influence to intimidate the Inspector.

Act One continued

Sheila enters and apologises for interrupting. The Inspector requests that she stays, but this angers Birling who threatens to report the Inspector. The Inspector tells Sheila that he's investigating the death of a young woman.

Gerald tries to shut the investigation down: *"we can't help you there because we don't know"*, but the Inspector suggests that it's not just Birling who is responsible for Eva's death.

> Comment: When Birling realises that someone else might be blamed for Eva's death, he's relieved (*"Well, of course, if I'd have known that earlier I wouldn't have called you officious"*). He doesn't care that someone's dead, or that his family might be involved, he's only concerned with saving his own reputation.

Sheila is the next member of the Birling family to be questioned by the Inspector

The Inspector explains that after Eva Smith was fired, she was unemployed for several months and struggling to get by. She was able to get a job as a sales assistant in an up-market clothing shop called Milwards, but after a few months, she was fired again. Birling comments that she must have been fired for *"Not doing her work properly"*.

> Comment: Birling is prejudiced towards the working class. He assumes that Eva is lazy or incompetent, even though he called her a *"good worker"* earlier.

The Inspector says that Eva was fired because a customer complained about her. Sheila asks what the girl looked like, and the Inspector shows her the photo. Sheila is shocked and exits the stage. Birling reprimands the Inspector for upsetting Sheila.

> Comment: It's ironic that Birling doesn't care that his actions led to Eva/Daisy dying by suicide, but he does care that the Inspector has upset Sheila. This shows how little Birling values the lives of the working class.

Gerald demands to see the photograph, but the Inspector refuses, *"cutting in, massively"*.

> Comment: It's suggested later in the play that the reason the Inspector refuses to show the photograph to more than one person at a time is because he has several photographs of different women, and he's combined Eva, Daisy and the woman calling herself 'Mrs Birling' into the same person.

Act One continued

Eric tells the Inspector that he intends to go to bed, but the Inspector tells him to stay. This implies that Eric may also be involved in Eva's suicide.

Comment: This increases the suspense for the audience as they are left to wonder who else is involved in her death.

Gerald tries to defend the family: *"we're respectable citizens and not criminals"*.

Comment: Gerald believes that he and the Birlings haven't committed any crimes, so they are 'good' people. This is an example of irony, as throughout the play, the Inspector examines the family's morals, and encourages the audience to judge for themselves whether the family are 'good' people. See **page 3** for more on morality plays.

Sheila returns and admits that she got Eva fired from Milwards. Sheila confesses that she was dress shopping and insisted on trying a dress that wouldn't suit her. When she tried it on, she recognised that she looked awful, and saw the shop assistants exchanging glances which made her feel humiliated, especially because Eva was very pretty. Sheila complained to the store owner, who fired Eva.

Comment: Just like Birling, Sheila used her privilege and influence to control people around her. For more on the character of Sheila, turn to **pages 35–36**.

Sheila feels remorse for her part in Eva's death

Act One continued

The Inspector says to Sheila: *"you might have been said to be jealous of her"*.

Comment: This links back to the play's genre as a morality play. Sheila represents the sin of envy. See **page 3** for more.

Sheila seems genuinely remorseful for her actions: *"I'll never, never do it again"*.

Comment: Sheila's remorse makes the audience more inclined to forgive her. It also suggests that some members of the middle class might be capable of learning from their mistakes and changing their ways.

The Inspector then reveals that Eva Smith changed her name to Daisy Renton. Gerald is *"startled"*, and pours himself a drink.

Comment: Gerald's reaction suggests that he is also involved in the death of Eva.

The Inspector and Eric exit, and Sheila confronts Gerald about his reaction to the name Daisy Renton. She assumes Gerald was involved with Daisy during the previous summer when he avoided Sheila. Gerald admits he knew Daisy, but begs Sheila not to mention it to the Inspector. Sheila replies: *"why — you fool — he knows."*

Comment: This exchange shows that Sheila is perceptive. It also shows a shift in the couple's relationship. Accusing Gerald of infidelity and calling him a *"fool"* suggests that Sheila is starting to stand up for herself.

The Inspector returns to the stage and asks, *"Well?"*

Comment: This line suggests the Inspector deliberately left Sheila and Gerald alone to encourage a confession. This gives the Inspector a sense of control and **omnipotence**: he knows everything.

The end of Act One marks a turning point in Gerald and Sheila's relationship

ACT TWO

In the second act, the Inspector turns his attention to Gerald and Mrs Birling.

Act Two

Act Two resumes where Act One left off, with the Inspector repeating, *"Well?"*

Comment: Restarting the play in the same place creates the sense that the Birlings' fate is inescapable.

Gerald tries to protect Sheila by excusing her from the rest of the questioning, but Sheila insists that she stays. Gerald assumes that Sheila wants to stay because she will enjoy seeing someone else go through the awkward questioning.

Comment: Sheila actually wants to stay because she no longer wants to hide from the real world. This shows her developing maturity.

Mrs Birling enters *"briskly and self-confidently"*. Mr Birling has told her why the Inspector is here, but she tells the Inspector: *"I don't think we can help you much"*.

Comment: Mrs Birling's behaviour suggests she has the same arrogance as her husband. She believes that their social standing will protect them from any accusations. For more information on the character of Mrs Birling, turn to **pages 32–34**.

Sheila warns her mother about lying to the Inspector, and Mrs Birling is surprised and frustrated by her daughter's behaviour. Mrs Birling comments, *"You seem to have made a great impression on this child, Inspector."* To which the Inspector replies, *"We often do on the young ones."*

Comment: The Inspector's comment suggests that this isn't the first time he's tried to influence someone's opinions on social responsibility, leaving the audience to wonder whether the Inspector has conducted an investigation like this before. This adds to his mysterious nature, see **pages 42–43**.

Mrs Birling tries to control the Inspector

Act Two continued

Just like Gerald, Mrs Birling tries to send Sheila to bed, but Sheila refuses.

Comment: Middle- and upper-class women were often shielded from anything unpleasant, whereas working-class women were not protected in the same way. This shows the inequality in how the classes were treated. For more on the theme of gender, see **pages 51–54**.

Mrs Birling comments that the Inspector is behaving in an *"offensive manner"*, and tries to use her husband's previous position as *"Lord Mayor"* and his role as *"magistrate"* to control the Inspector.

Comment: Mrs Birling tries to intimidate the Inspector, but he remains calm and *"imperturbable"*, suggesting he isn't frightened by their superior social position. For more on the character of the Inspector, turn to **pages 42–43**.

Mrs Birling tells the Inspector that Eric has had a bit too much to drink that evening. The Inspector insinuates that Eric has a drinking problem (*"some young men drink far too much"*) and Sheila confirms that Eric has been *"steadily drinking too much for the last two years"*.

Comment: Eric represents the sin of gluttony (excessive eating or drinking). For more on morality plays and the seven deadly sins, turn to **page 3**.

Mrs Birling is shocked to discover her son is an alcoholic: *"It isn't true... you must know it isn't true"*.

Comment: The fact that Eric has been able to hide his drinking for two years from his mother suggests that they don't have a very close relationship, or that Mrs Birling has been too self-involved to notice.

Birling enters, and says that Eric refuses to go to bed. The Inspector tells Birling that he wants to speak with Eric, but not now: *"He must wait his turn"*.

Comment: The Inspector has complete control of the investigation. He directs the family and says who he wants to speak to and when.

The Inspector turns his attention to Gerald, and asks when he first met Daisy Renton. Gerald admits that he met her in the Palace Bar, where he helped her escape the unwelcome advances of another man. Gerald recalls that she admitted to being very poor, so he found her somewhere to live and gave her some money.

The Inspector questions Gerald about his involvement with Eva/Daisy

GCSE **English Literature** | An Inspector Calls

Act Two continued

Eventually, she became his mistress. After a few months, the affair came to an end, and Daisy moved out of the accommodation that Gerald had provided for her. Upon recalling his relationship with Daisy, Gerald is so overwhelmed, he asks to leave the Birlings' house to get some air.

Comment: Gerald treated Daisy with care and affection, and seems to have genuine feelings for her. This presents Gerald in a more favourable light. For more on the character of Gerald, see **pages 40–41**.

The Inspector allows Gerald to leave, and Sheila gives Gerald her engagement ring back. Gerald exits the stage.

Comment: Although Sheila is angry that Gerald had an affair, she respects his honesty and how he treated Daisy with kindness, which shows her growing maturity. Sheila's decision to break off the engagement also shows her developing self-respect. She isn't prepared to marry a man who has been unfaithful, even if it was socially acceptable for an upper class man to have a mistress.

The Inspector turns his attention to Mrs Birling, and shows her a photograph of Eva/Daisy.

Mrs Birling claims she doesn't recognise the girl in photograph.

Comment: The Inspector knows that Mrs Birling is lying: *"You're not telling me the truth"*. He already knows the truth; he just wants to force confessions from the family.

Sheila implores her mother to admit that she knows the woman in the photograph: *"I know jolly well you did in fact recognise her"*.

Comment: Sheila is no longer a bystander. She has joined the Inspector in questioning her family.

The Inspector questions Mrs Birling about her involvement in Eva/Daisy's death

The audience hears the *"front door slam"*. Eric leaves the house.

Comment: Eric's exit symbolises his tendency to run away from his problems.

Mrs Birling admits that she sits on the board of the Brumley Women's Charity Organisation, and that two weeks previously a woman claiming to be called *"Mrs Birling"* came to ask for help.

Comment: The audience would recognise the hypocrisy of Mrs Birling belonging to a charitable organisation. She is not presented as a generous or kind person, instead her position with the charity is a way for her to have influence and power in the community.

Act Two continued

Mrs Birling admits that the woman using her name *"prejudiced"* her against the woman.

> Comment: Mrs Birling is offended that Eva/Daisy dared to use her name. Mrs Birling represents the sin of pride. See **page 3** for more on the seven deadly sins and morality plays.

Mrs Birling used her influence at the charity to prevent Eva/Daisy from receiving any help.

> Comment: Just like the other characters, Mrs Birling uses her power and authority to make Eva/Daisy suffer.

The Inspector reveals that Eva/Daisy came to the charity for help because she was pregnant.

> Comment: Eva/Daisy's pregnancy makes her death even more tragic.

Mrs Birling condemns the father of Eva/Daisy's unborn child

Eva/Daisy told Mrs Birling that she couldn't get help from the father of her child because he was *"only a youngster - silly and wild and drinking too much"* and that he'd given her stolen money that she wasn't prepared to accept any more. The Inspector encourages Mrs Birling to condemn the father of Eva/Daisy's unborn child. Mrs Birling agrees that *"he ought to be dealt with very severely"*.

> Comment: Sheila realises that the father is Eric before her mother does. This shows that Sheila is a perceptive character. Sheila tries to prevent Mrs Birling from saying any more, but Mrs Birling refuses to listen.

Mrs Birling finally realises that Eric was the father. The Birlings are *"terrified"* and *"agitated"*. Act Two ends with Eric entering the stage.

> Comment: Act Two ends with a revelation. This **climatic curtain** creates tension for the audience as they want to know how the situation will be resolved.

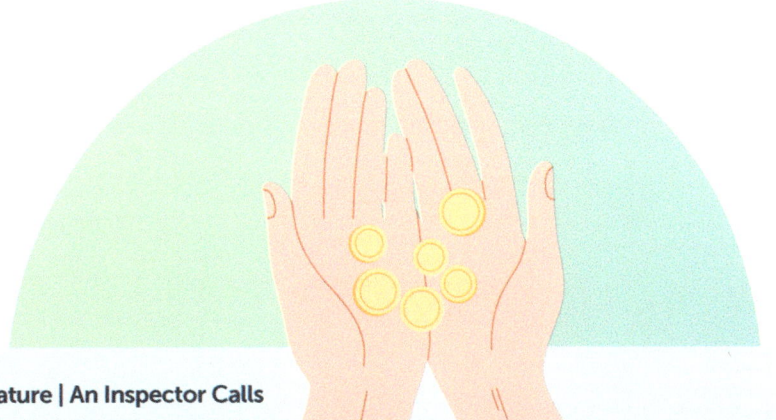

ACT THREE

Act Three is the final act. The Inspector questions Eric, and then leaves, giving the family an opportunity to reflect on their actions before the final twist.

Act Three

Comment: Act Three begins exactly where Act Two ended. This creates a sense that the Birlings' fate is inescapable.

Eric enters and says: *"You know, don't you?"*. He admits he was drinking at the Palace Bar, and he met Eva/Daisy and bought her some drinks.

Comment: It's implied that Eva/Daisy worked at the Palace Bar as a prostitute. The Palace Bar is a *"favourite haunt of women of the town"*, a **euphemism** for sex workers. The Birlings use euphemisms to disguise their language when they're talking about something unpleasant. This contrasts with the Inspector's language. He speaks plainly and bluntly.

Eva/Daisy got drunk because *"she'd not had much to eat that day"*.

Comment: This creates sympathy for Eva/Daisy. The audience know that she is poor and cannot afford to eat, and this allows Eric to take advantage of her.

Eric recalls that he went back to her lodgings, even though Eva/Daisy didn't want him to. Eric admits that he was in a state where *"a chap easily turns nasty"*, so Eva/Daisy let him in, and *"that's when it happened"*.

Comment: The revelation that Eric raped Eva/Daisy is shocking and appalling, and shows how little respect Eric had for her. For more on the theme of gender, see **pages 51–54**.

Birling tells Sheila and his wife to leave the room to protect them from the unpleasant details. Eric tells the Inspector that he met Eva/Daisy on several occasions and that she told him she was pregnant. Eric reveals he stole money from Birling's company to give to Eva/Daisy.

Comment: When Birling finds out that Eric stole the money, he says, *"I've got to cover this up"*. He doesn't care that Eva/Daisy and his unborn grandchild are dead, or that his son is a thief. He only cares about protecting his own reputation. Birling doesn't fire Eric for stealing from the company, but he did fire Eva/Daisy for asking for more money. This shows the double-standard in how the two characters were treated.

Eric admits that when Eva/Daisy discovered the money was stolen, she refused to take any more.

Comment: This shows that Eva/Daisy has very strong morals. Even though she is desperate for money, she's not prepared to break the law. For more on Eva/Daisy, see **pages 45–46**.

Act Three continued

The Inspector then reveals that Eva/Daisy went to Mrs Birling's charity to ask for money, but that she was turned away. Eric is devastated, and tells his mother, *"you killed her – and the child she'd have too – my child – your own grandchild"*.

Comment: This is one of the most emotional and distressing parts of the play. The earlier confessions steadily increase the tension leading up to this moment.

The Inspector gives his final speech, reminding the Birlings of their involvement in Eva/Daisy's death. The family's reactions are mixed. Sheila and Eric seem truly remorseful, whereas Birling tries to bribe the Inspector: *"Look, Inspector – I'd give thousands – yes, thousands-"*.

Comment: The younger members of the family, Sheila and Eric, give the audience hope that they will learn from this experience. For more on generational differences, see **pages 56–57**.

The Inspector reminds the family of their responsibility to other people in society. *"Eva Smith has gone – but there are millions and millions and millions of Eva Smiths and John Smiths"* and that *"We are members of one body"*.

Comment: The Inspector acts as Priestley's mouthpiece. He reminds the family, and the audience, about the importance of social responsibility. Priestley wants the audience to recognise that everyone deserves to be treated the same, irrespective of class and privilege.

The Inspector warns if members of society don't look after one another, *"then they will be taught it in fire and blood and anguish"*.

Comment: This could be a reference to the Second World War. When the play was first performed in 1945, World War II was just coming to an end. The death and devastation would have still been very fresh in the minds of audiences (see **page 9**). It could also be interpreted as having religious overtones. *"fire and blood and anguish"* may remind audiences of hell, implying that people who do not learn from his message could be punished in the afterlife.

Act Three continued

The Inspector leaves, and immediately Birling blames Eric. He's worried that there will be a *"public scandal"* which will affect his chances of receiving a knighthood.

Comment: Birling is still preoccupied with his public reputation. The Inspector's visit hasn't changed him.

Mr and Mrs Birling are *"subdued"* after the Inspector leaves

Sheila and Mrs Birling wonder whether the Inspector was a real police officer. Sheila remarks that it doesn't matter if he was a real police officer or not: the family still contributed to the death of Eva/Daisy. Mr and Mrs Birling think that if the Inspector was an imposter it *"Makes all the difference."*

Comment: Mr and Mrs Birling don't seem to have learnt anything from the Inspector's visit. Priestley could be commenting that the older generations are more resistant to change.

Birling reprimands the family for telling the Inspector so much: *"The fact is, you allowed yourselves to be bluffed"* and he comments that the Inspector was *"a Socialist"*.

Comment: The Inspector being called a *"Socialist"* is another clue that the Inspector is J. B. Priestley's mouthpiece. See **page 2** and **pages 8–9** for more on J. B. Priestley's political views.

Gerald returns, and tells the family: *"That man wasn't a police officer"*. Gerald recalls bumping into a police sergeant who told him there wasn't an Inspector Goole on the force. Birling rings the Chief Constable to confirm. Gerald and Mr and Mrs Birling are delighted that the Inspector wasn't real, and assume that the hoax was an attempt to discredit the family by one of Birling's rivals.

Comment: Just like the family, the audience is led to believe that the Inspector was a hoax. This makes the final twist even more shocking.

Mrs Birling congratulates herself for standing up to the Inspector *"I was the only one of you who didn't give in to him"*.

Comment: This reinforces Mrs Birling's prideful attitude.

Sheila and Eric are appalled by their parents' reactions, stating, *"This girl's still dead"*.

Birling, Gerald and Mrs Birling conclude that the Inspector showed them photographs of different girls, and that *"there wasn't the slightest proof that this Daisy Renton was really Eva Smith"*.

Comment: This isn't strictly true. When Gerald tells the Inspector about his affair with Eva/Daisy, he admits that she *"had a job in one of the works here"* and that she'd *"said something about the shop too"*. This suggests that Eva/Daisy were the same person, but Gerald, Birling and Mrs Birling want to ignore this, because it benefits them if there were several different girls.

Act Three continued

Gerald phones the infirmary

They decide to phone the infirmary to see whether a girl had died that evening by drinking bleach. The infirmary confirms that they haven't had a suicide in months. Gerald, Birling and Mrs Birling are relieved.

> **Comment:** They believe that it no longer matters how they treated Eva/Daisy because without a death, there won't be any negative consequences for the family.

Gerald, Birling and Mrs Birling pour drinks to celebrate uncovering the Inspector's hoax.

> **Comment:** The characters congratulating each other and pouring drinks mimics the moment just before the Inspector's arrival in Act One. It suggests that Gerald, Birling and Mrs Birling are reverting to their old behaviour.

Sheila and Eric are disturbed by their parents' attitude, and that they have learnt nothing.

> **Comment:** Some productions have Eric and Sheila stand near each other, but apart from Gerald, Birling and Mrs Birling. This visually represents the distance between the characters, and their differences in perspectives.

Gerald tries to make amends with Sheila and offers her the engagement ring.

> **Comment:** Sheila turns down the ring: *"No, not yet"*. This suggests that she is disappointed by his resistance to change, and symbolises her self-respect.

The telephone rings, and Birling is told that a girl has just died on her way to the infirmary after drinking disinfectant and that the police are on their way to ask the family some questions. The characters are left standing *"guiltily and dumbfounded"* as the curtain falls.

> **Comment:** The play ends with this final twist. The action is left unresolved and the audience wonder what will happen to the Birlings. Ending the play in this way suggests that the Birlings are stuck in a loop that they won't be able to escape until they all learn the importance of social responsibility.

CHARACTERS: MR BIRLING

Arthur Birling is the head of the Birling family. He is a *"prosperous manufacturer"* who has considerable influence in the local community, but he doesn't have a warm or close relationship with his family.

Comment: Birling is a **capitalist**: he's a businessman focused on making more money, often at the expense of others. He represents the opposite viewpoint to J. B. Priestley, who was a **socialist** and believed in the fairer distribution of wealth. Priestley portrays Birling in a negative way to encourage the audience to disagree with him and his views.

Act One

Ambitious: Birling is a member of the middle class, but has ambitions to become a member of the upper class. He married a woman who was his *"social superior"* and he's keen to impress Gerald, whose family are aristocrats, with talk of his knighthood.

Birling represents capitalism

Comment: Birling is more concerned with his social standing than being a good person. His desperation to impress people suggests that he's insecure.

Pompous: Birling makes a long-winded speech at dinner, concentrating on his own thoughts and self-interests rather than celebrating his daughter's engagement.

Comment: Priestley establishes Birling's arrogant and self-important nature at the very beginning of the play. This makes him an unlikable character.

Greedy: Birling is delighted with his daughter's engagement to Gerald because he hopes he can work with Gerald's family's company for *"lower costs and higher prices"*.

Comment: Birling sees the engagement as a business deal, and Sheila is a commodity that he can use for his own benefit. For more on the theme of gender, see **pages 51–54**.

Foolish: Birling responds to rumours about war by saying *"there isn't a chance of war"*. This creates dramatic irony as the audience know that the First World War will start two years later.

Comment: This shows that Birling has poor judgement. If he's wrong about the war, then he could be wrong about other things too, such as the importance of social responsibility.

Patronising: Birling says women like clothes because it's something *"to make 'em look prettier"* and a *"token of their self-respect"*.

Comment: Birling views fashion as inconsequential, and he associates women with fashion. He thinks women are only interested in 'trivial' things. He also objectifies women by commenting on their appearance. This attitude was fairly typical at the time, where women were expected to look pretty and be obedient. See **pages 51–54** for more on the theme of gender.

Mr Birling, Act One, continued

Birling is presented as an unsympathetic character

Selfish: Birling comments that *"a man has to... look after himself"*. He doesn't agree with *"cranks"* who believe in the importance of *"community"*.

> **Comment:** Birling rejects the idea of social responsibility. He sees socialism as a threat to his wealth and status. For more on the theme of social responsibility, see **page 47**.

Arrogant: Birling tries to assert his dominance over the Inspector by mentioning he was an alderman (local councillor) and Lord Mayor. Birling thinks highly of himself, and he believes reminding the Inspector of his social status will offer him some protection or special treatment.

> **Comment:** Priestley shows how some members of the upper and middle class try to use their privilege for their own benefit and to make themselves feel important.

Controlling: Birling wants to be in charge, and isn't used to being confronted. He's frustrated that the Inspector is taking control, and Birling speaks to the Inspector *"with a touch of impatience"*.

> **Comment:** As the boss of a company and the head of the family, Birling is used to being in charge, and he's annoyed someone socially inferior to him is taking charge in his own home.

Unrepentant: Birling doesn't recognise his role in Eva's death: *"I can't accept any responsibility"*.

> **Comment:** Since he hasn't broken the law, Birling believes his actions were excusable (see **page 3** for more on morality and legality). However, this makes Birling seem heartless and callous, and the audience is likely to criticise his attitude.

Prejudiced: Birling views Eva/Daisy as *"cheap labour"*, and after he sacks her, he asks what happened to her: *"Get into trouble? Go on the streets?"* He assumes that, since she's working class, she would turn to crime.

> **Comment:** Birling's attitude towards the working class would have been representative of some people from the upper and middle classes at the time. Working-class people were unfairly viewed by some as worthless, lazy and without morals. See **page 5** for more.

Protective: When the Inspector shows Sheila the photograph and it upsets her, Birling is angry: *"Why the devil do you want to go upsetting a child like that?"*

> **Comment:** It's ironic that Birling wants to protect his daughter from the unpleasantness of seeing the photo, but he's indifferent to the suffering that Eva went through. This shows the inequality between how middle-class and working-class women were treated.

Act Two

Unlike his children, Birling doesn't change during the play. He shows a lot of the same traits in Acts Two and Three as he does in Act One.

Threatening: When the Inspector refuses to question Eric immediately, Birling responds: *"I don't like your tone or how you're handling this enquiry"*.

Comment: Birling believes he's the Inspector's social superior, so he tries to use his authority to intimidate the Inspector.

Alarmed: Birling is *"terrified"* when he realises that Eric was the father of Eva/Daisy's unborn child.

Comment: Priestley uses exclamations and an unfinished sentence to show Birling's shock at the revelation: *"My God! But – look here-"*.

Act Three

Enraged: Birling is furious at Eric's relationship with Eva/Daisy, and his confession that he stole money. He speaks to Eric *"explosively"*, *"harshly"* and *"savagely"*.

Comment: Birling wants to cover up the stolen money *"as soon as I can"*. He's more concerned with a *"public scandal"* damaging his business than he is about Eva/Daisy's death.

Desperate: Birling tries to bribe the Inspector. *"I'd give thousands – yes, thousands-"*.

Comment: Birling tries to use his wealth and privilege to protect himself.

The final twist is revealed when Birling receives a phone call from the police

Unwilling to change: By the end of the play, Birling doesn't seem to have learnt anything from the Inspector's visit. *"There's every excuse for what both your mother and I did — it turned out unfortunately, that's all-"*.

Comment: Neither Birling nor his wife appear to change following the Inspector's visit. Birling just wants things to go back to how they were.

Triumphant: When Gerald phones the infirmary and discovers that no young women have been brought in, Birling is delighted that it was all a hoax: *"Nothing but an elaborate sell!"*

Comment: Birling wants the Inspector's visit to be a hoax so he doesn't have to acknowledge his part in Eva/Daisy's death.

Distressed: Birling receives the telephone call at the very end of the play informing him that a police officer is on his way. He's described as being *"panic stricken"*.

Comment: Birling's fear gives the audience hope that maybe this time he will learn to take responsibility for his actions.

How far does Priestley present Mr Birling as a selfish character?

Write about:
- what Mr Birling says and does
- how far Priestley presents Mr Birling as a selfish character.

[30 + 4 marks]

Your answer may include:

AO1 — show understanding of the text
- *Birling is delighted by his daughter's engagement to Gerald because it benefits him. He sees their marriage as a business deal, rather than something which will make his daughter happy. Gerald's family are from the upper class, so being associated with the Crofts will benefit Birling's social standing, and their marriage will also contribute to "lower costs and higher prices" which will make Birling richer.*
- *He doesn't believe in looking after other members of society: a man must "look after himself" and he calls socialists "cranks". This shows how Birling only cares about himself.*
- *Birling refuses to pay Eva/Daisy more money because paying his workers more would damage his profits. Birling only acts in a way that will benefit himself.*
- *When it's revealed that other family members will be questioned about Eva/Daisy's suicide Birling is relieved. He speaks with a "marked change of tone" and apologises. He doesn't care that his family might also be involved, he's only concerned about his reputation.*
- *When the Inspector leaves, Birling doesn't seem to have learnt anything and he never shows any genuine sympathy towards the death of Eva/Daisy or his unborn grandchild. He's more concerned that there will be a "public scandal" and that his knighthood might be in jeopardy.*

AO2 — show understanding of the writer's language choices
- *Birling has several monologues in Act One. This shows how Birling thinks his thoughts and opinions are more important that anyone else's.*
- *Birling often calls other people's opinions "rubbish" and "nonsense". He's close-minded and unwilling to see things from a different perspective than his own.*
- *Birling resents how the Inspector challenges his authority. He often speaks to the Inspector "angrily" and tries to interrupt or intimidate him.*
- *An Inspector Calls follows the format of morality plays and Birling represents the sin of greed.*

AO3 — relate the play to the context
- *Birling represents capitalism and the privileged middle class. He doesn't want the class structure to change because he benefits from exploiting the working class.*
- *Birling also represents a patriarchal and misogynistic society. As the head of the Birling family, he believes he has authority over his wife and daughter. He sees Sheila as a commodity that he can benefit from.*

This answer should be marked in accordance with the levels-based mark scheme on page 61.

Make sure your answer to this question is in paragraphs and full sentences. Bullet points have been used in this example answer to suggest some information you could include. There are four marks available for spelling, punctuation and grammar, so make sure you read through your answer carefully, correcting any mistakes.

CHARACTERS: MRS BIRLING

Mrs Birling is the wife of Mr Birling and the mother of Sheila and Eric. She's prejudiced towards the working class, and shows no remorse towards the death of Eva/Daisy.

Act One

Proper: She tells Birling off for complimenting the cook, (*"Arthur, you're not supposed to say such things"*), reproaches Sheila for using the word *"squiffy"*, and tells Birling *"I don't think you ought to talk business on an occasion like this."*

Comment: Mrs Birling is preoccupied with etiquette; she wants her family to act a certain way, and she's not afraid to scold them if they don't behave in the way she expects. This presents Mrs Birling as cold and formal.

Mrs Birling is her husband's *"social superior"*

Traditional: Mrs Birling tells Sheila that she must *"get used to"* Gerald spending nearly all *"his time and energy"* on work.

Comment: Mrs Birling upholds the patriarchal system where women were expected to be subservient to men. See **pages 51–54** for more on the theme of gender.

Mrs Birling exits the stage before the Inspector arrives and doesn't re-enter until Act Two.

Act Two

Disdainful: Mrs Birling disapproves of the Inspector, and accuses him of conducting himself in a *"peculiar and offensive manner"*.

Comment: Mrs Birling isn't afraid to criticise the Inspector because she believes she's better than him. She reminds the Inspector that her husband was *"Lord Mayor only two years ago"*. Like Birling, she thinks that her family's social status will intimidate the Inspector.

Untruthful: She lies about not recognising the photo of Eva/Daisy.

Comment: Later in the Act, Mrs Birling admits that she refused to help Eva/Daisy because Eva/Daisy told Mrs Birling *"a pack of lies"*. This presents Mrs Birling as hypocritical: she punishes Eva/Daisy for lying, but Mrs Birling is also a liar.

Mrs Birling, Act Two, continued

Petty: Mrs Birling refuses to help Eva/Daisy because she used the name *"Mrs Birling"*, and she prejudices the other committee members against Eva/Daisy.

Comment: Mrs Birling is offended when Eva/Daisy uses the name 'Mrs Birling' in connection with being pregnant and unmarried. Mrs Birling represents the sin of pride. See **page 3** for more on morality plays.

Uncooperative: Initially, Mrs Birling refuses to answer any more of the Inspector's questions: *"I prefer not to discuss it any further, you have no power to make me change my mind"*.

Comment: Mrs Birling thinks that her social standing means she's above the law, and can be protected from answering the Inspector's questions. However, because of her pride, Mrs Birling is unable to resist defending her actions.

Unsympathetic: The Inspector suggests that Eva/Daisy and Mrs Birling had common ground: *"You've had children. You must have known how she was feeling"* but Mrs Birling doesn't have any sympathy towards Eva/Daisy, commenting: *"you're quite wrong to suppose I shall regret what I did."*

Comment: Even though Mrs Birling has some shared experiences with Eva/Daisy, she can't empathise with her. Because Eva/Daisy is working class, Mrs Birling can't recognise that they would ever have something in common. Mrs Birling's lack of sympathy towards Eva/Daisy makes her unlikable which encourages the audience to disagree with her perspective.

Prejudiced: Mrs Birling judges Eva/Daisy because she is working class: *"As if a girl of that sort would ever refuse money!"*

> Mrs Birling implies that Eva/Daisy is greedy because she wouldn't refuse money, but it's ironic that she doesn't recognise her own husband's greed for exploiting *"cheap labour"*.

Comment: Mrs Birling believes that someone's position in society is indicative of whether they are a 'good' person. Mrs Birling believes that upper- and middle-class people are automatically 'good' whereas working-class people are automatically 'bad'. Mrs Birling's attitudes towards the working class were typical for the time. For more on the class system, turn to **pages 4–6**.

Refuses to take responsibility: Mrs Birling attempts to push the blame on to the father of Eva/Daisy's unborn child (*"he ought to be dealt with very severely"*).

Comment: Mrs Birling sees the father of Eva/Daisy's child as a scapegoat. She thinks that he is ultimately responsible for Eva/Daisy's death, rather than herself. She is unwittingly blaming Eric, which creates dramatic irony.

Act Three

Distressed: When Eric realises his mother turned Eva/Daisy away, he exclaims: *"Then – you killed her."* Mrs Birling is upset: *"No – Eric – please – I didn't know."*

Comment: Mrs Birling's dialogue is usually very composed, so this fragmented speech shows her distress.

Judgemental: Mrs Birling's feelings of distress and guilt towards Eric don't last long. After the Inspector leaves, she turns on her son and says *"I'm absolutely ashamed of you"*.

Comment: Rather than trying to make amends, the Birling family descend into bickering and blaming each other.

Mrs Birling is distressed when she discovers that Eric is the father of Eva/Daisy's unborn child

Smug: When the family believe the Inspector was a fake, Mrs Birling comments: *"I was the only one of you who didn't give into him."*

Comment: Rather than reflecting on the seriousness of the situation, Mrs Birling is more preoccupied with gloating. This highlights her prideful nature. See **page 3**.

Resistant to change: Just like her husband, Mrs Birling doesn't appear to have changed following the Inspector's visit: *"from the way you children talk, you might be wanting to help him* [the Inspector] *instead of us."*

Comment: Priestley presents the older generation as unwilling to change. See **pages 56–57** for more on the theme of generational differences.

CHARACTERS: SHEILA

Sheila is the daughter of Mr and Mrs Birling. She's in her *"early twenties"* and engaged to Gerald Croft. She learns from the Inspector's visit, and she changes by the end of the play.

> Sheila is in her *"early twenties"* and Eva/Daisy is *"Twenty-four"*. Despite their similar age, their lives are very different. Priestley suggests that a person's fate is dictated by the class they are born into.

Act One

Childish: Sheila's language in Act One shows her youth. She calls her parents *"Mummy"* and *"Daddy"*.

Comment: Priestley makes Sheila seem immature at the beginning of the play to emphasise just how much her character changes and matures by the end of the play.

At the start of the play, Sheila is presented as a privileged young woman

Perceptive: Sheila knows that something wasn't quite right with Gerald the previous summer. Even when he claims he was just busy at work, Sheila replies: *"Yes, that's what you say"*, suggesting she doesn't believe him.

Comment: This foreshadows Gerald's later revelation that Gerald was having an affair with Daisy.

Sympathetic: Sheila sympathises with Eva: *"these girls aren't cheap labour – they're people"*.

Comment: Sheila's compassion hints that she might be more receptive to the Inspector's message about social responsibility.

Privileged: She shops at a *"good"* department store for clothes.

Comment: This contrasts with the Inspector's image of women like Eva/Daisy *"counting their pennies in their dingy little back bedrooms"*. This description highlights the inequality between the different social classes.

Devastated: Sheila is distraught by her involvement in Eva/Daisy's suicide. She *"almost breaks down"* when she recounts what happened.

Comment: Sheila's genuine remorse makes the audience feel more sympathy towards her, and presents her as a forgiveable character.

Envious: Sheila had Eva/Daisy fired out of jealousy, just for suiting the dress better than she did.

Comment: Sheila represents the sin of envy. See more about morality plays on **page 3**.

GCSE **English Literature** | An Inspector Calls

Act Two

Stubborn: Even after the Inspector has finished questioning her, she refuses to leave.

> **Comment:** Sheila doesn't want to be protected from the 'real world' anymore. She begins to show maturity and acknowledge the inequality faced by others. Although Gerald and her parents keep trying to protect her from the unpleasantness, Sheila refuses to conform to societal expectations of a 'delicate female'.

Remorseful: Sheila acknowledges her guilt: *"I know I'm to blame – and I feel desperately sorry"*.

> **Comment:** This suggests that Sheila will be able to learn from the Inspector's visit and change for the better.

Dignified: She listens to Gerald's story about his affair with Eva/Daisy, and although she's hurt by it, she handles it in a mature way. After Gerald confesses, she tells him: *"I rather respect you more than I have ever done before"*.

> **Comment:** Sheila appreciates Gerald's honesty and the kind way that he treated Eva/Daisy. This shows how she's considering other people beyond her own feelings.

Inquisitive: Sheila joins the Inspector in questioning the rest of the characters, and encourages their confessions: *"Were you in love with her, Gerald?"*

> **Comment:** Unlike Mr and Mrs Birling, Sheila isn't concerned with protecting her family's reputation or hiding their secrets. She just wants to discover the truth.

Mature: She recognises that the Inspector's visit has changed her. She remarks to Gerald: *"You and I aren't the same people who sat down to dinner"*.

Blunt: Sheila is shocked by her mother's refusal to help Eva/Daisy: *"I think it was cruel and vile"*.

> **Comment:** Sheila's behaviour towards her parents begins to shift. She starts to criticise them, and recognise their flaws. For more on the theme of generational differences, see **pages 56–57**.

Act Three

Able to change: Sheila seems the most affected by the Inspector's visit, and seems willing to change: *"I remember what he said, how he looked, and what he made me feel"*.

Frustrated: She criticises her parents and Gerald when they don't appear to have learnt from the Inspector's message: *"You began to learn something. And now you've stopped"*.

> **Comment:** Sheila also starts to rebel against traditional female expectations. She argues with her parents and breaks off her relationship with Gerald. She gives the audience hope that things can change for the better. For more on the theme of gender, see **pages 51–54**.

How far does Priestley present Sheila as a character who changes her attitudes towards herself and others during the play?

Write about:
- what Sheila says and does throughout the play
- how far Priestley presents Sheila as a character who changes her attitude towards herself and others.

[30 + 4 marks]

> *Your answer may include:*
>
> *AO1 — show understanding of the text*
> - *At the start of the play, Sheila is introduced as a vapid and immature middle-class woman. She doesn't listen to her father because she's "admiring her ring", and later in Act One Eric comments that Sheila and Mrs Birling were "talking about clothes again". This presents her as materialistic and preoccupied with inconsequential things.*
> - *Sheila is engaged to Gerald even though she's suspicious about his behaviour the previous summer. She chooses to ignore her doubts about him, suggesting that she is prepared to overlook any unpleasantness. This is reinforced when she learns about Eva/Daisy's suicide as she tells the Inspector: "I wish you hadn't told me". She wants to be protected from reality.*
> - *As Act One progresses, Sheila begins to change. She speaks out against her father using the working class as "cheap labour" and realises how the working class are exploited by the upper and middle classes.*
> - *She shows remorse when she realises the consequences of having Eva/Daisy fired from Milwards: "I'll never, never do it again."*
> - *She refuses to leave the room when the Inspector questions other members of the family. She no longer wants to be protected from the truth.*
> - *She develops self-respect and calls off the engagement to Gerald when she realises that he has been unfaithful and shows little remorse for his involvement in Eva/Daisy's death.*
> - *She rejects her parents' attitudes towards social responsibility and challenges them: "you don't seem to have learnt anything".*
>
> *AO2 — show understanding of the writer's language choices*
> - *Priestley shows Sheila's youth at the start of the play with her language choices. She calls her parents "Mummy" and "Daddy", and she uses slang like "squiffy".*
> - *As the play develops, Sheila seems to join forces with the Inspector, questioning and challenging members of her family. She uses, blunt, direct language: "Mother, I think it was cruel and vile" and challenges Gerald calling him a "fool".*
>
> *AO3 — relate the play to the context*
> - *At the start of the play, Sheila represents stereotypes around privileged, spoiled middle-class women. She is preoccupied with material things and protected from unpleasantness. However, as the play progresses, Sheila seems to break away from these stereotypes. She challenges the patriarchal system by confronting her father and refusing the engagement ring in Act Three.*
>
> *This answer should be marked in accordance with the levels-based mark scheme on page 61.*

> ⭐ Make sure your answer to this question is in paragraphs and full sentences. Bullet points have been used in this example answer to suggest some information you could include. There are four marks available for spelling, punctuation and grammar, so make sure you read through your answer carefully, correcting any mistakes.

CHARACTERS: ERIC

Eric is the Birlings' son. He's hiding a drinking problem, and a relationship with Eva/Daisy. Although he's not a likable character, he seems to learn from the Inspector's visit, which suggests he will change for the better.

Act One

Drunk: Eric's behaviour during dinner implies that he's been drinking. He *"suddenly guffaws"*, suggesting he's not quite in control of himself, and Sheila says he's *"squiffy"*.

Comment: Priestley hints at Eric's drinking problem so that the audience connects him with the father of Eva/Daisy's unborn child who was *"wild and drinking too much"* in Act Two.

Eric's drinking problem is hinted throughout the play

Nervous: Gerald jokes that Eric has *"been up to something"*. Eric is defensive, replying: *"(uneasy) Well, I don't think it's very funny"*. This hints that Eric is hiding something.

Comment: This is an example of **foreshadowing**. Eric's uneasy because he's hiding his drinking problem as well as his relationship with Eva/Daisy, and her pregnancy.

Sympathetic: When Birling admits that he fired Eva for asking for higher wages, Eric is sympathetic towards her, saying *"I think it's a dam' shame"*.

Comment: Eric's sympathetic attitude towards Eva and the strikers presents him more favourably, and suggests he will be more receptive to the Inspector's message. Eric points out his father's hypocrisy: *"Why shouldn't they try for higher wages? We try for the highest possible prices"*. This highlights to the audience that Eva's behaviour isn't that dissimilar from Birling's, but that she was unfairly punished for it because of her class.

Act Two

As Birling's son, Eric comes from a family with a lot of money and influence. Eric abuses this position by drinking and *"going round the town"*, and assumes that his family name will protect him from a scandal.

Comment: Eric is off-stage for a lot of Act Two. This allows the audience and the rest of the family to hear Mrs Birling's confession about refusing to help Eva/Daisy. Eric's absence allows the tension to build without revealing the twist that he is the father of Eva/Daisy's child.

Alcoholic: Sheila reveals that Eric has been *"steadily drinking too much for the last two years"*.

Comment: The fact that Eric has been able to hide his drinking from his parents suggests that they don't have a good relationship: his parents haven't noticed his drinking, and Eric doesn't think he can ask them for help.

Act Three

Agitated: When Eric enters in Act Three, he's distressed because everyone knows about his secret relationship with Eva/Daisy. He lashes out at Mrs Birling: *"You haven't made it any easier for me"*.

Comment: Eric tried to keep his relationship with Eva/Daisy a secret because it would be unacceptable for a middle-class man to have a public relationship with a working-class woman.

Rapist: Eric rapes Eva Smith (*"she didn't want me to go in but that – well, I was in that state when a chap easily turns nasty"*).

Comment: While audiences today recognise that Eric raped Eva/Daisy, audiences at the time might have been more lenient towards Eric's confession, partly because Eva was a prostitute, and partly because she was working class. There was a belief that working-class women involved in sex work were less deserving of sympathy in matters of sexual assault.

Misogynistic: Eric describes Eva as *"pretty and a good sport"*, suggesting that he liked her because she was attractive and obedient. He describes other sex workers as *"fat old tarts"*. Eric doesn't have much respect for working-class women. Turn to **page 54** for more on Eric's attitude to women.

Misguided: When Eric finds out that Eva/Daisy is pregnant with his child, he tries to help her by offering her money. However, the money is stolen from his father's business.

Comment: Eric's efforts to help Eva/Daisy make him seem more sympathetic to the audience. He didn't abandon her when he found out she was pregnant.

Eric blames his mother for the death of his unborn child

Unsupported: Eric doesn't have a good relationship with his father. Eric admits to Birling that *"you're not the kind of father a chap could go to when he's in trouble"*.

Comment: Although Eric has done some terrible things, the audience recognises that he is the product of his environment, and that his parents are partially to blame for his upbringing.

> Eric has a job at Birling's factory. This is an example of **nepotism** (when someone with power gives a friend or relative special treatment).

Devastated: Eric is distraught when he realises Mrs Birling refused Eva/Daisy help: *"You killed them"*.

Comment: Eric's emotional response contrasts with his parents' indifference.

Remorseful: Eric feels guilty and takes responsibility for his actions: *"we all helped to kill her"*.

Comment: Like Sheila, Eric seems to have learned from the Inspector. Even when it's suggested that the Inspector could have been a hoax, Eric doesn't forgive himself for what he has done.

CHARACTERS: GERALD

Gerald is Sheila's fiancé. His parents are Lord and Lady Croft, so he's the Birlings' social superior and represents the upper class in the play. Like Mr and Mrs Birling, Gerald is unchanged by the Inspector's visit.

Act One

Suspicious: Sheila questions Gerald about his whereabouts last summer when he wasn't around very much, and he responds: *"I was awfully busy at the works"*.

Comment: Sheila's doubts about Gerald hint that he isn't entirely trustworthy. Sheila's suspicions are confirmed when Gerald reveals he was having an affair with Eva/Daisy.

Capitalist: When Birling suggests to Gerald that their businesses should work together for *"lower costs and higher prices"*, Gerald agrees, saying *"Hear, hear!"*

Comment: Birling and Gerald share a few similarities, specifically their approach to business. This hints that Sheila is going to marry someone similar to her father, and that her future looks very similar to that of her parents'. This suggests that it could be difficult for upper- and middle-class people to change their outlooks, because they were surrounded by people who held similar views.

Comfortable: He has a good relationship with Birling, who tells him *"You're just the kind of son-in-law I always wanted."* Birling confides in him about the knighthood, and they agree on business and politics. Gerald is respectful towards Birling, even though Gerald is socially superior, calling him *"sir"*.

Comment: Birling seems to like Gerald more than his own son. It could be because Gerald's a *"well-bred young man"* who will provide social connections and business opportunities.

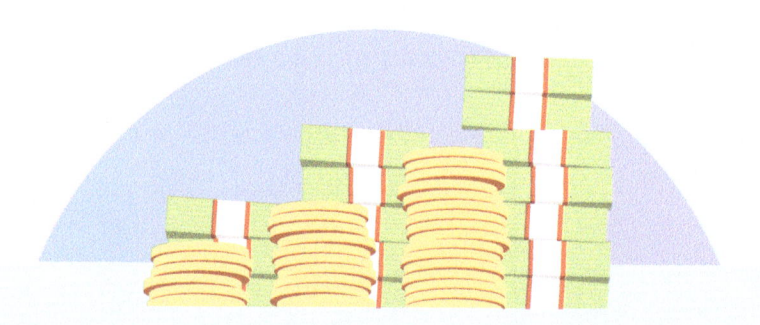

Gerald and Sheila are engaged at the start of the play

Act Two

Patronising: He tries to speak on Sheila's behalf: *"I think Miss Birling ought to be excused any more of this questioning... She's had a long, exciting and tiring day"*.

Comment: Gerald speaks about Sheila as if she were a child. This also shows how middle- and upper-class women were often shielded from unpleasantness as they were thought to be too sensitive to be able to cope.

Hypocritical: Gerald calls the town's Alderman a *"rogue"* and a *"womaniser"*. However, he doesn't recognise that using prostitutes and being unfaithful also makes him a womaniser.

Comment: Gerald thinks that he 'saves' Eva/Daisy from men at the bar, but he also uses and exploits her.

Misogynistic: Gerald refers to some of the prostitutes who work at the Palace Bar as *"hard-eyed dough-faced women"*. He believes a woman's worth is tied to her appearance.

The Inspector reveals Gerald's affair with Eva/Daisy

> Gerald buys sex workers, but he also shows a lack of respect towards them. For more information on Gerald's attitude towards women, turn to **page 54**.

Kind: He seemed to care for Eva/Daisy and he found her a place to live and gave her money. He admits he's *"upset"*, and he's so affected by her death he asks to leave the house.

Comment: Despite his kindness towards Eva/Daisy, Gerald was in full control of the relationship and broke it off when it no longer suited him. Eva/Daisy was homeless and unhappy when he ended their affair. This highlights the power that the upper classes had over the working classes, as well as the power that men had over women in relationships.

Act Three

Perceptive: Gerald is the first to suggest that the Inspector could have been asking questions about several different girls: *"We've no proof it's the same photograph and no proof it's the same girl"*.

Comment: Rather than face up to what he has done, Gerald tries to undermine the Inspector's investigation to make himself feel better.

Unwilling to change: Just like the older Birlings, Gerald doesn't seem to have learnt anything from the Inspector's visit. After they discover a women hasn't died in the infirmary that night, he tells Sheila, *"Everything's all right now"*. He thinks everything can just go back to normal.

Comment: Although the younger characters, Sheila and Eric, appear to learn from the Inspector's visit, Gerald behaves more like the older generation and is resistant to change.

CHARACTERS: THE INSPECTOR

The Inspector drives the action of the play by investigating Eva/Daisy's death and questioning the other characters.

The Inspector is J. B. Priestley's mouthpiece. Priestley uses the Inspector to convey his thoughts about social responsibility to the audience as well as the characters.

Act One

Comment: The Inspector's name is Goole. This sounds like the word 'ghoul' (another word for 'ghost'). This hints at the Inspector's almost supernatural nature, see **page 43**.

Outsider: The Inspector doesn't belong to the Birlings' world, and he doesn't attempt to fit in. He refuses a drink (*"No, thank you, Mr Birling. I'm on duty."*) and he doesn't play golf.

Comment: The Inspector doesn't seem to belong to a class. He isn't part of the Birlings' privileged world, so he's able to criticise it without being hypocritical, but he isn't working class either.

The Inspector interrupts the Birlings' celebration

Blunt: The Inspector deliberately uses direct, emotive language to provoke a reaction: *"Burnt her inside out"*. This contrasts with the Birlings' polite, euphemistic language.

Comment: The Inspector makes the characters uncomfortable. Birling speaks to the Inspector *"angrily"* and he makes Sheila feel *"distressed"*. This is a departure from the celebratory scene at the start of the play, where the family are relaxed and *"pleased with themselves"*.

Forceful: The Inspector interrupts the other characters, *"cutting through, massively"*. He's not intimidated by the Birlings' social status, and disregards how he's 'supposed' to behave.

Comment: The rigid class structure of the 1910s meant that people of the upper and middle classes would have expected to be treated with respect by their inferiors. The Inspector is unwilling to confirm to this social etiquette.

Biased: It's clear from the outset that the Inspector is biased against the Birlings, and that he's willing to judge their actions. When Birling admits that he fired Eva/Daisy for asking for higher wages, the Inspector says: *"it's better to ask for the earth than to take it"*.

Comment: The Inspector is meant to be a police officer, however, no crime has been committed. Even though the Birlings have treated Eva/Daisy poorly, they haven't broken the law. Despite this, the Inspector still holds them accountable for Eva/Daisy's death. This makes the characters and the audience questions whether he is a genuine police officer.

The Inspector, Act One, continued

Authoritative: The Inspector is in full control of the investigation. He prevents other characters from seeing the photo, and he questions the Birlings and Gerald in a specific order.

Comment: This also allows the play's narrative to unfold chronologically which makes it easy for the audience to understand the consequences of each of the character's actions.

Omnipotent: During the questioning, the Inspector doesn't find out anything he didn't already know. Instead, he uses his visit to force confessions from the family members and make them aware of their role in Eva/Daisy's suicide.

Comment: The Inspector's omnipotence is also a useful dramatic technique. It allows him to make revelations which progress the action and create tension.

Act Two

Comment: The Inspector's characterisation is largely consistent across the play. He doesn't change or develop, but his emotions become more intense.

Impatient: *"Don't stammer and yammer at me again, man. I'm losing all patience"*.

Comment: In Act One, the Inspector called Birling *"sir"*, now he's shouting at him and calling him *"man"*. This shows that the Inspector has lost all respect for Birling.

Cunning: He allows Mrs Birling to unwittingly blame Eric for Eva/Daisy's death: *"No hushing up, eh? Make an example of the young man, eh?"*

Comment: Priestley uses the Inspector to create **dramatic irony**. The audience recognises Eric is the father before Mrs Birling does.

Act Three

Supernatural: The Inspector warns the characters about *"fire and blood and anguish"*. This could be a prediction of World Wars I and II, which implies that the Inspector can see into the future.

Comment: J. B. Priestley wanted to adhere to the naturalistic style of theatre, so he was careful not to make the Inspector too obviously supernatural. If the Inspector had been presented as a ghost, it could have distracted from the serious message Priestley wanted to impart.

Mysterious: At the end of the play, it's not clear whether the Inspector is real or a hoax. Gerald confirms that the Inspector doesn't work for the local police force, so it's not clear how the Inspector knows about Eva's death and the Birlings' involvement.

Comment: The Inspector's mysterious identity may make the audience feel as though he could reappear in their lives if they don't respect others.

How does Priestley use the Inspector to explore ideas about responsibility?

Write about:
- what the Inspector says and does
- how Priestley uses the Inspector to explore ideas about responsibility. [30 + 4 marks]

Your answer may include:

AO1 — show understanding of the text
- The Inspector is used as a dramatic device to question the Birling family, and to reveal how they were each partly responsible for Eva/Daisy's death. The Inspector shows the "chain of events" that drove her to suicide.
- As well as admitting how they were involved with Eva/Daisy's death, the Inspector wants the characters to take responsibility for what happened, and to change their ways.
- The Inspector doesn't behave like a real police officer. He is not impartial, instead he is vocal about the Birlings' actions and passes judgement on them. Even though Gerald and the Birlings didn't directly kill her, the Inspector believes they have behaved immorally towards her, and are responsible for her death.
- The Inspector's final speech is focused on how people "are responsible for each other". He wants the characters, and the audience, to understand how a person's actions have consequences.

AO2 — show understanding of the writer's language choices
- The Inspector is omnipotent. He knows exactly what the family have done, and his omnipotence allows him to press the characters when they lie or hide the truth. For example, Mrs Birling initially refuses to acknowledge that she recognises Eva/Daisy in the photograph, but the Inspector insists "You're not telling me the truth."
- The Inspector uses blunt language to shock the characters and the audience: "she lies with a burnt-out inside on a slab". This makes Eva/Daisy's death seem more visceral and real, and forces the characters to understand the consequences of their actions.
- The Inspector's final speech uses Biblical language of "fire and blood and anguish" as a warning if people do not learn compassion towards each other. This imagery would also have been very powerful for audiences in the 1940s who were just emerging from World War II.

AO3 — relate the play to the context
- The Inspector acts as Priestley's mouthpiece. Priestley was a socialist who believed that the class system was unfair, and that wealth should be distributed more evenly. The older characters and Gerald are resistant to the Inspector's message of social responsibility, as they benefit from exploiting the working class. However, Sheila and Eric seem to learn from the Inspector's message, suggesting that the younger generation may be more receptive to socialist ideas than the older generations.

This answer should be marked in accordance with the levels-based mark scheme on page 61.

> Make sure your answer to this question is in paragraphs and full sentences. Bullet points have been used in this example answer to suggest some information you could include. There are four marks available for spelling, punctuation and grammar, so make sure you read through your answer carefully, correcting any mistakes.

CHARACTERS: EVA/DAISY

The entire play revolves around Eva/Daisy, but she never appears on stage. She is a powerless victim of an unfair patriarchal class system. It's not certain whether Eva/Daisy are the same person, or several different women.

Comment: The name 'Eva Smith' symbolises her role as a working-class 'everywoman'. 'Eve' was the first woman according to the Bible, and 'Smith' was the most common British surname.

Act One

Comment: In Christian teachings, people who died by suicide were thought to be sent to hell. This shows just how desperate Eva/Daisy was to escape her life.

Eva/Daisy doesn't have any dialogue, and we only discover more about her through the other characters. This represents how the working class were voiceless and unable to speak out against the way they were treated.

Working class: Eva/Daisy works in Birling's factory, and then as a shop assistant.

Comment: Birling sees Eva/Daisy as *"cheap labour"*. Priestley highlights how the upper and middle classes exploit the working classes for their own benefit.

Hard-working: Birling describes her as a *"good worker"* who was due to be promoted.

Comment: Eva's hard-working nature means the audience is more sympathetic to her when they discover Birling sacked her.

Outspoken: Eva organises a strike to ask for better wages. She is prepared to stand up for herself.

Comment: In the 1910s, some women were campaigning for women's rights, such as the suffragettes. Outspoken women were often derided, usually by powerful men, so Eva/Daisy's attempts to stand up for herself show her strength of character.

Hopeless: After Eva/Daisy is fired from Birling's factory, she's *"lonely, half-starved"* and *"desperate"*.

Comment: This creates pity for Eva/Daisy, and shows how difficult it was for working-class people to break the cycle of poverty.

Anonymous: Eva Smith changes her name to Daisy Renton. The surname *"Renton"* hints at her job as a sex worker and how she 'rents' her body.

Comment: The Birling family are proud of their name. Birling's business is called *"Birling and Company"* and Mrs Birling is insulted when Eva/Daisy uses the name *"Mrs Birling"*. However, Eva/Daisy changes her name because her identity is worthless.

Act Two

> The Inspector reveals that Eva/Daisy left a letter and *"a sort of diary"*. This allows the Inspector to reveal some of Eva/Daisy's thoughts and feelings. It also helps to explain how the Inspector knows so much about her.

Loving: Eva/Daisy's relationship with Gerald appears to be genuine. She was *"happier than she'd ever been before"*. After Gerald breaks off the affair, Eva/Daisy left town to *"be quiet and remember"* their relationship.

> **Comment:** Eva/Daisy is presented as heartbroken, whereas Gerald seems to move on easily. This creates sympathy for Eva/Daisy.

Powerless: During her affair with Gerald, it's clear that he controls their relationship. He was the one who ended their relationship, suggesting that she didn't have any say in the matter.

> **Comment:** Gerald uses Eva/Daisy when it suits him. As soon as the affair is over, he discards her and makes her homeless. This highlights the power imbalance in their relationship.

Act Three

> During Eric's confession it's implied that Eva/Daisy was involved in sex work. This suggests that she has run out of alternative ways to make a living.

Desperate: Eva/Daisy pretends her 'husband' has left her to try to get help from the charity.

> **Comment:** Eva/Daisy knows she will be judged if she admits she is pregnant and unmarried.

Moral: Eva/Daisy refuses Eric's stolen money, even though she needs it.

> **Comment:** Eva is presented as more honourable than the other characters. Priestley wanted to show that being a 'good' person isn't dictated by someone's social class.

CHARACTERS: EDNA

Edna symbolises the working class

Edna is the Birling's parlourmaid. She reminds the audience of the Birlings' wealth and privilege.

Dutiful: Edna has very few lines in the play, but the lines she does have are spoken politely, and are related to serving the Birlings: *"Yes, ma'am"*.

> **Comment:** Edna is the only working-class character to appear on stage, but she says very little. She serves as a visual reminder of the working class, and how their voices are oppressed by the upper and middle classes.

THEMES: SOCIAL RESPONSIBILITY

J. B. Priestley believed in social responsibility: the idea that everyone in society should look after each other.

J. B. Priestley's message

Social responsibility is the most important theme in *An Inspector Calls*. Priestley uses the play to explore how the actions of the upper and middle classes can affect the lives of the working class. Priestley wanted audiences to accept that they have a responsibility to help those around them, and to show how the working class were exploited by their social superiors and trapped in a cycle of poverty, which was very difficult to break.

> Comment: Going to the theatre was popular among the upper and middle classes. Priestley wrote a play so he could target these groups with his message about social responsibility.

Exploiting the working class

All the characters exploit or mistreat Eva/Daisy in some way.

Mr Birling

Mr Birling pays Eva/Daisy very little, and sees her as *"cheap labour"*. He fires her from his factory when she tries to stand up for herself. Losing her job leaves her *"half-starved"* and *"desperate"*.

Eric

Eric uses his position as a middle-class man to buy sex from Eva/Daisy, and he rapes her. He hides her pregnancy from his family (who could have afforded to help her) because she was working class.

Sheila

Sheila uses her influence as a good customer at Milwards to have Eva/Daisy sacked. After being fired from two jobs, it's implied that Eva/Daisy became a prostitute to support herself.

Gerald

Gerald hides his relationship with Eva/Daisy because it would have damaged his reputation. Gerald uses his connections to find her somewhere to live, but he withdraws this when it doesn't suit him anymore and she's left homeless.

Mrs Birling

Mrs Birling abuses her power at the charity to punish Eva/Daisy because she is angry that Eva/Daisy used her surname.

> Comment: When Eva/Daisy loses her job at Birling's factory and Milwards, she doesn't have many options. She doesn't have any family to support her, and in the 1910s, the government didn't provide benefits for the unemployed. Eva/Daisy highlights the need for a welfare state to help those who are struggling. In 1945, when the play was first performed, the Labour Party planned to introduce more government aid, such as the National Insurance scheme, which provides money for the unemployed, the elderly and those on maternity leave (see **page 9**).

Attitudes towards social responsibility

The Inspector

The Inspector tries to teach the family about the importance of social responsibility, and the significance of looking after other people, especially those who are less fortunate. He tries to show how a *"chain of events"* led to Eva/Daisy's suicide, and that the family must share the blame for her death. In his final speech, the Inspector warns society will suffer if people do not learn compassion towards each other.

> Comment: The Inspector's final speech can be compared to Birling's speech in Act One. Where Birling rejects the idea of social responsibility and is (wrongly) optimistic about the future (*"There'll be peace and prosperity… everywhere"*), the Inspector warns of *"fire and blood and anguish"* in the future. Audiences in 1945 would have recognised that the Inspector was correct, alluding to the death and devastation caused by World War I and II.

Buildings destroyed by bombing in London during World War II

Some characters don't change

Mr Birling

Birling represents capitalism: the idea of making money at the expense of others. He thinks that a man should *"look after himself"*, and that socialists are *"cranks"*. He doesn't believe in helping others because he wants to protect his own interests. Keeping the working class poor benefits Birling because they provide *"cheap labour"*, while making him rich. Birling refuses to change because social inequality works for him.

> Comment: Birling represents the opposite view to Priestley. Priestley makes Birling an unlikable and foolish character (he believes *The Titanic* is *"unsinkable"*) so that audience members would want to distance themselves from Birling's attitude towards social responsibility.

Birling's disdain for socialism was probably fairly representative of the upper and middle classes during 1910s. For many people, it would take two World Wars to convince them to change their minds. See **pages 4–9** for more on socialism and the class system.

Mrs Birling

Mrs Birling is openly prejudiced towards the working class. She remarks *"As if a girl of that sort would ever refuse money!"* She believes that working-class people are to blame for their own misfortunes, and doesn't recognise how difficult it is to escape from the cycle of poverty. It's ironic that she serves on a charity committee when she uses her position to cause suffering, rather than to help. Priestley could be suggesting that if the working classes had to rely on the charity of the upper and middle classes, they would be unlikely to get the help they needed. She doesn't learn from the Inspector's visit, even after she contributed to the death of her grandchild.

Some characters don't change, continued

Gerald

Gerald has a similar attitude to the working class as Birling. When Birling admits that he fired Eva/Daisy for asking for higher wages, Gerald agrees: *"You couldn't have done anything else"*. Gerald is also prejudiced towards the working class, viewing them as financially irresponsible: *"They'd be all broke — if I know them"*. Gerald shows some remorse for Eva/Daisy's death, but doesn't seem to change his outlook towards social responsibility. When he believes that the Inspector was a hoax, he expects things to go back to normal. Gerald thinks his actions are excusable since he didn't suffer any negative consequences.

Comment: Although Gerald is a similar age to Eric and Sheila, unlike them, he is resistant to the Inspector's message about social change. Priestley could be commenting that the upper classes would be more intolerant to change than the middle classes because they had more to lose from social equality.

Other characters seem able to change

Sheila

At the start of the play, Sheila is ignorant about the working class. As a privileged middle-class woman, she has little understanding of the difficulties faced by those who are poorer than her. Sheila gets Eva/Daisy fired from her job, but doesn't recognise the consequences of her actions at the time. When the Inspector explains the repercussions of Eva/Daisy losing her job, Sheila shows remorse and seems inclined to change: *"I'll never, never do it again"*. As well as recognising that she wants to change, Sheila rejects her parents for not learning from the Inspector's visit.

Comment: Sheila represents how Priestley wanted audience members to react to his message about social responsibility.

Eric

Like Sheila, Eric leads a privileged life, and he seems unaware of the difficulties faced by the working class. His main interactions with the working class are at the Palace Bar where he buys sex. As the Inspector reveals more about Eva/Daisy's life, Eric seems sympathetic to the working class. *"It's what happened to the girl and what we all did to her that matters."*

Comment: Priestley presents the younger generation as being more sympathetic to the idea of social responsibility and more receptive to change.

How does Priestley explore the importance of social responsibility in *An Inspector Calls*?

Write about:
- some ideas about social responsibility in the play
- how Priestley presents the importance of social responsibility. [30 + 4 marks]

Your answer may include:

AO1 — show understanding of the text

- The Birling family represent the middle class, and Gerald represents the upper class. Priestley shows their privilege by describing their dining room as "heavily comfortable" with props of "champagne glasses" and a "decanter of port". On the other hand, Eva/Daisy represents the working class. She is described as "half-starved" and "penniless". The difference between the groups highlights the inequality of society during this period, and the need for change.

- Birling believes a man must "look after himself", and he mocks "cranks" who believe in social responsibility. Priestley uses dramatic irony to portray Birling as foolish. For example, Birling believes The Titanic is "unsinkable". This encourages the audience to laugh at Birling and question Birling's views on social responsibility, because if he is wrong about The Titanic, he is likely to be wrong about other things too.

- Throughout the play, the characters are all shown to have exploited or hurt Eva/Daisy in some way, eventually leading to her suicide. The characters did not realise the consequences of their actions at the time, and this causes the audience to question their own actions to consider whether they could have unknowingly contributed to another person's misery.

- The younger characters, Sheila and Eric, appear to learn from the Inspector's message, and this gives the audience hope that people can change and work towards a fairer society.

AO2 — show understanding of the writer's language choices

- In the Inspector's final speech, he warns that if society doesn't learn about the importance of social responsibility, they will be taught in "fire and blood and anguish". This shocking language would have reminded audiences in the 1940s of World War II.

- Gerald, Birling and Mrs Birling do not change following the Inspector's visit, and they want things to return to normal. At the very end of the play, the revelation that a girl has died in the infirmary implies that history will keep repeating itself until the Birlings' acknowledge that society is unfair and that it needs to change.

AO3 — relate the play to the context

- Priestley was a socialist and he believed in a fairer society where the working classes weren't exploited by the upper and middle classes. He uses the character of the Inspector as a mouthpiece to convey his beliefs about society to the audience.

- In 1945, society was beginning to change in part due to World War II. Much of British society wanted the government to provide benefits and healthcare to those in need. This led to a landslide victory by the Labour Party following the war.

This answer should be marked in accordance with the levels-based mark scheme on page 61.

Make sure your answer to this question is in paragraphs and full sentences. Bullet points have been used in this example answer to suggest some information you could include. There are four marks available for spelling, punctuation and grammar, so make sure you read through your answer carefully, correcting any mistakes.

THEMES: GENDER

Society in 1910 was patriarchal: men had authority both at home and in the community. Priestley uses *An Inspector Calls* to suggest that the younger generation were starting to move towards a more equal society.

The women

Sheila

At the start of the play, Sheila conforms to female stereotypes of the time. She's childish (referring to her parents as *"Mummy"* and *"Daddy"*) and seems preoccupied with material possessions (she admires her ring, and says: *"isn't it a beauty?"*).

Sheila appears to be a model daughter, who is doing her duty by marrying well. She's careful to present herself as submissive and docile. For example, when she questions Gerald about his absence the previous summer she is *"half serious, half playful"*. Sheila knows that as Gerald's subordinate, she can't confront or accuse him directly, so she must do it in a *"playful"* way to avoid being seen as disrespectful or aggressive.

Sheila is jealous of Eva/Daisy's beauty, and this is partly why she has Eva/Daisy fired from her job. This reinforces Sheila as petty, shallow and envious; characteristics that were often associated with women.

As the play develops, Sheila matures and begins to show signs of independence. She insists on staying to listen to the Inspector's investigation, even when Gerald and her father try to excuse her from the unpleasant details. After the Inspector questions Sheila and she admits her part in firing Eva/Daisy from Milwards, the power balance between her and Gerald shifts. This could be because Sheila is beginning to mature and understand the reality of social inequality. Sheila mocks and challenges Gerald. She talks to him with *"sharp sarcasm"* and presses him about his affair with Eva/Daisy: *"Were you in love with her, Gerald?"*. She challenges her parents and their views on social responsibility and she turns down the engagement ring, which suggests that she isn't prepared to settle for someone who has been unfaithful and who cannot admit their mistakes and learn from them.

Gerald tries to protect Sheila from hearing anything unpleasant

Comment: Sheila gives the audience hope that the younger generation will continue to fight for female equality.

The women, continued

Eva/Daisy

Eva/Daisy shows signs of breaking away from traditional gender roles. She's a *"ring-leader"* of the strikes at Birling's factory, suggesting that she wasn't afraid to speak out against injustice. Birling hints that she was outspoken *"she had a lot to say – far too much"* and this assertive behaviour led to him firing her, showing how men at this time often wanted to silence opinionated women.

When Eva/Daisy falls pregnant and goes to Mrs Birling's charity for help, Eva/Daisy pretends to be *"a married woman who had been deserted by her husband"*. Eva/Daisy knows that she needs to lie about her situation, because the committee would be less sympathetic to an unmarried, single woman. This highlights the gender taboo surrounding women who had sex outside of marriage, even though men like Gerald and Eric could have extra-marital sex without facing judgement.

Eva/Daisy highlights the difficulties faced by working-class women

While Sheila is provided for and protected by the men in her life (Birling, Eric and Gerald), Eva/Daisy is abused and exploited by them. She is at the mercy of Birling, Eric and Gerald at various points in the play, which shows that even outspoken women could easily be repressed by powerful men, and how a woman was treated was often dependant on her social class.

Mrs Birling

Mrs Birling represents female stereotypes of the period. She perpetuates traditional gender roles, telling Sheila that men *"spend nearly all their time and energy on their business"*, and implying that she expects Sheila to know her place and to continue to uphold these values.

> **Comment:** This shows how the patriarchal system was passed down from generation to generation, and how difficult it was to challenge or question.

Although Mrs Birling is her husband's *"social superior"* she recognises that he is head of the household. Mrs Birling assumes that Birling will take control of situations: *"just be quiet so that your father can decide what we ought to do"*. Mrs Birling is happy to defer to her husband, rather than make decisions for herself. Mrs Birling accepts traditional gender roles and doesn't want to question or challenge them. Priestley suggests that upholding traditional gender stereotypes can be damaging. Mrs Birling shows no sympathy towards Eva/Daisy when she discovers that she's an unmarried, single mother. Having sex outside of marriage was stigmatised for women, and Mrs Birling punishes Eva/Daisy for lying about being deserted by her husband by refusing to give her any charity.

The men

The Inspector

The Inspector treats the female characters similarly to the male characters. He doesn't try to protect them or patronise them, for example, he doesn't shy away from using unpleasant language in front of them. He describes how Eva/Daisy *"lies with a burnt-out inside on a slab"* to Mrs Birling and Sheila. The Inspector defends Eva/Daisy. He doesn't judge her, and he doesn't agree with the way that the characters treat her for being female and working class.

Comment: The Inspector judges people based on whether they are 'good', rather than their class or gender.

The Inspector treats the male and female characters equally

Mr Birling

Mr Birling represents the traditional patriarchal society. He's the head of the family, the breadwinner and has influence in the local community. As a result, he expects respect from his family and doesn't like his authority to be challenged. When Eric questions Birling's opinions on war, Mr Birling impatiently interrupts: *"Just let me finish, Eric"*.

Birling is delighted with Sheila and Gerald's engagement because it will benefit his own business. This shows how his daughter's happiness is secondary to his own ambitions, and he sees Sheila as a possession that he can leverage for his own benefit.

Mr Birling is misogynistic. He thinks that women are shallow and preoccupied with insignificant things. He remarks that women see clothes as a *"token of their self-respect"*. He believes that a woman's worth is tied to her appearance.

Birling is protective of Sheila and Mrs Birling, and he tries to shield them from unpleasantness. When the Inspector shows Sheila the photo of Eva/Daisy, Birling says: *"Why the devil do you want to go upsetting the child like that?"* It's ironic that he's angry that his daughter's upset, but isn't angry about Eva/Daisy dying by suicide. This highlights how middle-class women were seen as more valuable than working-class women.

When it's revealed that Gerald has had an affair, Birling seems to take Gerald's side *"But you must understand that a lot of young men-"*, implying that he can forgive Gerald for being unfaithful to his daughter because affairs were tolerated amongst men.

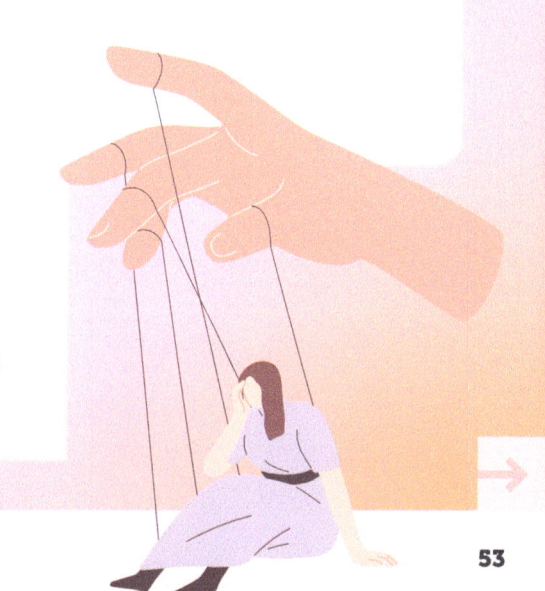

GCSE **English Literature** | An Inspector Calls

The men, continued

Eric

Eric represents how misogynistic views were passed down from generation to generation. Eric echoes Birling's comments about women being *"potty"* about clothes, reinforcing the idea that women are viewed as shallow and materialistic.

He buys sex from working-class women, which shows how upper-class and middle-class men often exploited women in hopeless situations. He talks disparagingly about the women in the Palace Bar, calling them *"fat old tarts"*, which reinforces the misogynistic belief that a woman's value is dependant on youth and beauty.

Comment: Priestley highlights the hypocrisy of upper- and middle-class men. They were disdainful of sex workers, while secretly using them.

Eva/Daisy takes her own life by drinking disinfectant. This could be read as symbolism for the way she may have wanted to clean herself after being violated by men like Eric and Gerald.

Gerald

Although Gerald isn't as overtly misogynistic as Eric or Birling, he still upholds traditional stereotypes. He tries to protect Sheila by excusing her from the Inspector's investigation: *"She's nothing more to tell you. She's had a long, exciting and tiring day"*. Gerald patronises Sheila, describing her as if she is a child. He speaks on her behalf, suggesting he has control over her, and is the person who decides what is best for her.

Like Eric, it's also implied that Gerald uses prostitutes. This shows the double-standard of how upper- and middle-class women were supposed to remain virgins before marriage, whereas it was acceptable for men to sleep around.

Birling and Gerald represent a patriarchal society

Comment: Gerald describes the sex workers as *"hard-eyed, dough-faced women"*. Gerald objectifies women, and cares more about a woman's appearance than her personality.

Gerald is in complete control during his relationship with Eva/Daisy. He tells the Inspector *"I became at once the most important person in her life"*. This shows Gerald's sense of self-importance and how he viewed Eva/Daisy as submissive to him. Although Gerald treats Eva/Daisy with kindness, he drops her when it suits him, leaving her homeless.

How does Priestley use Eva/Daisy to explore ideas about gender in *An Inspector Calls*?

Write about:
- how Eva/Daisy is treated by the other characters
- how Priestley uses Eva/Daisy to explore ideas about gender.

[30 + 4 marks]

Your answer may include:

AO1 — show understanding of the text
- As a single, working-class woman, Eva/Daisy is at the bottom of the social hierarchy in 1910. Priestley explores how damaging the patriarchal system is, by showing how Eva/Daisy is exploited and repressed by Gerald and the Birling family.
- In the 1910s, women were expected to be submissive and polite. Priestley presents Eva/Daisy as breaking away from these stereotypes. She asks for better pay and is a "ring-leader" of the strikes at Birling's factory, which suggests she was prepared to stand up for herself. However, she is punished for her actions by losing her job. This shows how difficult it was for women to confront inequality.
- Eva/Daisy is used and exploited by the men in the play. Birling sees her as "cheap labour", Gerald keeps her as his mistress, and Eric rapes her. Priestley shows how women like Eva/Daisy were treated with little respect, especially by upper- and middle-class men.
- Eva/Daisy is also repressed by the female characters. Eva/Daisy recognises that as an unmarried, pregnant woman, she will be stigmatised by the women at Mrs Birling's charity. Therefore, she pretends her husband has deserted her to make her story more sympathetic. Priestley shows how women could be prejudiced towards other women, because expectations surrounding women were passed down from generation to generation and entrenched in society.

AO2 — show understanding of the writer's language choices
- Eva/Daisy is never seen on stage, but she represents working-class oppression. Her story is told by the other characters, which symbolises how working-class women were voiceless, and had little control over their lives.
- Priestley presents Eva/Daisy as a blameless character. For example, even though she is "hard-working" she is unfairly dismissed from two jobs. Priestley wanted to highlight how some women suffered through no fault of their own, and how difficult it was for women to escape the cycle of poverty, especially when they were mistreated by others in society.

AO3 — relate the play to the context
- Society in 1910 was patriarchal, and women were expected to behave differently to men. For example, Eva/Daisy would have been judged for falling pregnant outside of marriage, whereas men, such as Gerald and Eric, had the freedom to sleep around outside of marriage and face no consequences for their actions. Eva/Daisy decides to kill herself rather than deal with the difficulties of being a single, unmarried woman, which shows how challenging being a working-class woman could be.

This answer should be marked in accordance with the levels-based mark scheme on page 61.

Make sure your answer to this question is in paragraphs and full sentences. Bullet points have been used in this example answer to suggest some information you could include. There are four marks available for spelling, punctuation and grammar, so make sure you read through your answer carefully, correcting any mistakes.

THEMES: GENERATIONAL DIFFERENCES

At the start of the play, everyone knows their place in the Birling family structure. However, the Inspector's visit causes a rift between the older and younger generations.

Before the Inspector arrives

At the start of Act One, Birling has authority over the younger characters. As a self-made businessman who has learnt from the *"school of experience"*, Birling thinks he knows better than the younger generation. In his speech, he tries to impart his 'knowledge' to Sheila, Eric and Gerald, but his language is often patronising and condescending, telling them *"You've a lot to learn yet"*, how *"things are so much easier"* for young people, as well as referring to Sheila, Gerald and Eric as *"youngsters"*.

Before the Inspector arrives, the family seem content and everyone knows their place

Comment: Birling's speech shows how he tries to influence the younger generation's thoughts and opinions.

Mrs Birling also has authority over the younger characters. She scolds her family for not behaving in a 'proper' way, for example she tells Sheila off for using the term *"squiffy"*. She tries to impose her traditional beliefs about the role of women on her daughter. For example, she explains to Sheila that she should get used to the idea of Gerald being busy with work.

The younger generation show respect to their elders. Sheila apologises for being distracted by her ring (*"I'm sorry, Daddy"*) and Gerald frequently refers to Birling as *"sir"*. None of the younger characters challenge Mr and Mrs Birling: they know their place in the family hierarchy.

Comment: Before the Inspector arrives, it seems as though the younger Birlings will follow in their parents' footsteps, and they will lead very similar lives to their elders.

After the Inspector arrives

After the Inspector exposes the family's secrets, he drives a wedge between the two generations and the family dynamic starts to deteriorate.

Initially, the generational differences are minor, for example, Eric and Sheila show more compassion and sympathy towards Eva/Daisy than their parents.

> Comment: Priestley shows a gradual division between the older and younger characters. Sheila and Eric slowly change their outlook which is more believable than a sudden change.

When it's revealed that Birling fired Eva/Daisy for asking for more money, Eric questions *"Why shouldn't they try for higher wages?"*. However, Gerald takes Birling's side (he *"couldn't have done anything else"*) which foreshadows Gerald taking Mr and Mrs Birling's side after the Inspector leaves.

As the Inspector's investigation progresses, Mr and Mrs Birling seem unwilling (or incapable) to change their outlooks. Priestley might be commenting that the older generation could be stubborn, and often refused to listen to the younger generation. For example, even when Sheila tries to warn her mother about the Inspector's questioning, Mrs Birling shuts her down: *"I don't know what you're talking about, Sheila"*.

By the end of the play, the parents and children speak very differently to one another. They no longer use respectful language; they speak *"angrily"* and *"bitterly"*, suggesting how hostile the relationship has become. Sheila and Eric challenge their parents' perspectives on Eva/Daisy's death, and are frustrated and angry by their parents' inability to learn from the Inspector's visit.

On the other hand, Mr and Mrs Birling condescend and undermine their children's feelings: *"They're over-tired. In the morning they'll be as amused as we are"*, assuming that they will change their minds. When Eric and Sheila show no sign of backing down, Birling instead tries to mock their views towards social responsibility, calling them *"the famous younger generation who know it all"*.

> Comment: The younger Birlings give hope that society will change for the better in the future, but Priestley implies that they might face resistance from the older generations.

Mrs Birling disregards her daughter's thoughts about social responsibility

GCSE **English Literature | An Inspector Calls**

EXAMINATION PRACTICE

1. How far does Priestley present Eric as irresponsible in the play?
   Write about:
   - what Eric says and does
   - how Priestley presents Eric as irresponsible. [30 + 4 marks]

2. How far does Priestley present society as unfair in *An Inspector Calls*?
   Write about:
   - what can be seen as unfair in the play
   - how Priestley presents society as unfair. [30 + 4 marks]

3. When the Inspector forces Mrs Birling to confess to her involvement in Eva/Daisy's death, Mrs Birling says, *"But I accept no blame for it all"*.
   How far does Priestley present Mrs Birling as someone who only cares about herself and her family?
   Write about:
   - what Mrs Birling says and does
   - how far Priestley presents Mrs Birling as someone who only cares about herself and her family. [30 + 4 marks]

EXAMINATION PRACTICE ANSWERS

1. Eric is presented as a privileged middle-class man. He comes from a wealthy family, and has a *"public-school-and-Varsity"* life. It's implied that he has benefited from nepotism, and has a job at his father's company at the *"works"*. This suggests that he is fortunate, and things have come easily to him in life: he doesn't know what it means to be out of work or to struggle financially. This portrayal was probably fairly representative of middle-class young men in the 1910s, who benefited from a patriarchal class system, which saw men with money as the most powerful individuals in society. Some would argue that as a powerful young man, Eric had a duty to behave sensibly and responsibly, and has a lot to lose by being reckless. However, Eric abuses his power and privilege, which ultimately leads to the death of Eva/Daisy. Priestley wanted to highlight that the class system was inherently unfair, especially because it was often abused by those who behaved irresponsibly.

   Priestley presents Eric as spoiled and reckless from the very start of the play. During Act One, it's clear that he's *"squiffy"* and is behaving oafishly, telling everyone at the dinner that Sheila has a *"nasty temper"*. This foreshadows the unpleasant behaviour that Eric confesses to later in the play.

   When the Inspector arrives, Eric tries to excuse himself from the questioning: *"I think I'd better turn in"* and in Act Two the audience hears the *"door slam"* and Birling confirms that Eric has left the house. This symbolises how Eric tries to run away from his problems, rather than facing them, which hints at his irresponsible behaviour towards Eva/Daisy which is revealed in Act Three.

   In the final Act, it's disclosed that he spends time *"going round the town"*, drinking and looking for prostitutes in the Palace Bar. His reckless and irresponsible behaviour have led him to develop a drinking problem, and he's been *"steadily drinking too much for the last two years."* His alcoholism causes him to rape Eva/Daisy, and he admits that he forced his way into her lodgings because he *"threatened to make a row"*. It's revealed that Eric's relationship with Eva/Daisy resulted in an unwanted pregnancy. At this point, the audience can clearly see how Eric's reckless behaviour has brought misery to Eva/Daisy, but as a middle-class man he can easily walk away from the situation, whereas Eva/Daisy must deal with the consequences. Although Eric recognises that he has an obligation to help her, he once again acts irresponsibly. Rather than asking his family for help, or earning money to support her, Eric decides to steal from his father's business. Ultimately, Eva/Daisy discovers that the money is stolen, and refuses to take any more. This leads to a chain reaction, where Eva/Daisy is forced to look elsewhere for help. She describes Eric as *"silly and wild and drinking too much"* which suggests that Eva/Daisy herself considers Eric as irresponsible and a poor father to her child. Since Eva/Daisy cannot rely on Eric, this leads to her to be rejected by Mrs Birling's charity, and eventually kill herself. This suggests that if Eric had been able to support Eva/Daisy lawfully, she wouldn't have been forced to take her own life, so Eric's reckless behaviour indirectly led to Eva/Daisy's death.

   By the end of the play, Eric seems to acknowledge his part in Eva/Daisy's death and take responsibility for his actions. He admits, *"the girl's dead and we all helped to kill her"*. This gives the audience hope that Eric will learn from his behaviour, and start to take more responsibility for those around him, particularly those who are less privileged.

2. Priestley presents society as unfair in *An Inspector Calls*, both in terms of the unfair class system that dominated British society at the time, but also the unfair patriarchal system that oppressed women. The most obvious way that Priestley demonstrates this combination of working class and female repression is through the character of Eva/Daisy, who is abused and exploited by Gerald and the Birling family because she is both working-class and female. However, towards the end of the play, the audience is given hope that things may improve.

   Priestley presents the Birling family as privileged. The men wear *"tails and white ties"* to dinner, and the family are drinking *"champagne"*. This highlights the family's comfort and affluence. In contrast, Eva/Daisy is described as *"hungry"* and *"almost penniless"*, which shows the enormous difference between the middle and working classes at the time. Sheila and Eva/Daisy are a similar age, however, their lifestyles are very different. Sheila doesn't need to work because her family will provide for her, and she spends her time shopping for nice clothes at Milwards. On the other hand, Eva/Daisy needs to work to survive. Priestley shows how a person's future is dictated by the class they are born into, which is inherently unfair.

   Priestley shows, through a chain of events, how Eva/Daisy is mistreated by Gerald and the Birling family. Although Eva/Daisy's experiences are probably exaggerated for dramatic effect, they were representative of how some working-class people were treated at the time. For instance, Eva/Daisy is sacked from Birling's company for asking for more money and she is fired from Milwards at Sheila's request. This shows how the working class were often at the mercy of the middle class, and how much power middle-class people had over working-class people. In both these instances, Eva/Daisy is left destitute, and has no government support to help her get back on her feet. On the other hand, when it's revealed that Eric has stolen fifty pounds from his father's company, he is not sacked. This shows how working class people could be dismissed for very minor things, whereas the middle classes, who also benefited from nepotism, would not be punished in the same way.

   Eva/Daisy is treated unfairly outside of the workplace too. After being fired from two jobs, she turns to sex work to support herself. When she works as a prostitute, she is again exploited by those around her. Eric has so little respect for Eva/Daisy because she is working class, that he forces himself on her and rapes her. If Eric had raped an upper- or middle-class women, he probably would have been punished. However, because he raped a working-class women, Eva/Daisy doesn't report it, so Eric doesn't face any consequences for his actions. After Eric gets her pregnant, it is Eva/Daisy who must take responsibility for supporting their unborn child. Again, this shows how working-class people were unfairly left to deal with the consequences of their social superiors, even though it would be far more difficult for her to raise a child.

In conclusion, Priestley uses the play to show how both women and the working class were treated unfairly in this period. However, following the Inspector's visit, Eric and Sheila recognise their part in Eva/Daisy's death and acknowledge that she was treated unfairly by all members of the family. They show a willingness to change and learn from their mistakes, which gives the audience hopes that things will change for the better. Audiences watching the play in 1945 would have just emerged from the Second World War, and following the war there was a national feeling that society needed to become fairer. The Labour Party, who represented the working classes, won a landslide victory and began introducing reforms such as National Insurance and the NHS to provide more support for those who needed it. Priestley wanted audiences to understand that these societal changes would help *"the millions and millions and millions of Eva Smiths and John Smiths"*.

3. Priestley presents Mrs Birling as a character who only cares about herself and her family. She represents the conservative upper class who were resistant to the Inspector's message about social responsibility. The wealthy elite were critical of socialism, because they benefited from keeping the working class poor. Priestley presents Mrs Birling as self-centred and unlikable so that audience members find her, and her outlook, unappealing.

   When Mrs Birling first meets the Inspector, she tells him: *"I don't think we can help you much"*, even though she knows that the Inspector is investigating a death, she attempts to dismiss the Inspector so that the family can continue their celebrations. She doesn't seem to care that someone has died and that she might be able to help the enquiry, instead she sees the Inspector as an unpleasant inconvenience.

   When the Inspector starts questioning Mrs Birling, she lies about recognising the photograph of Eva/Daisy, even though Sheila knows *"jolly well you did in fact recognise her"*. Mrs Birling's lie could be interpreted as her trying to protect herself from the investigation: she may suspect that she's involved somehow, but that she doesn't want to admit to any involvement. This once again shows how Mrs Birling doesn't care about the investigation into Eva/Daisy's death; her main concern is protecting herself from the investigation.

   As well as lying about the photograph, Mrs Birling continues to be uncooperative, and refuses to answer the Inspector's questions. This shows how she doesn't respect Eva/Daisy enough to allow the Inspector to do his job. Mrs Birling gives the impression that she is above the law, and tries to intimidate the Inspector with her social standing and her husband's role as *"Lord Mayor"*. Mrs Birling thinks that her position in society will protect her from the Inspector.

   When the Inspector finally forces her to confess, Mrs Birling admits that she refused to give Eva/Daisy any charity because Eva/Daisy called herself *"Mrs Birling"*. Mrs Birling is outraged by the *"impertinence"*, and this prejudices Mrs Birling against Eva/Daisy. This highlights how Mrs Birling places her own pride and reputation above the suffering and misery of Eva/Daisy. This suggests that although Mrs Birling sits on a charity committee, she only does so because it benefits herself by giving her power and influence, rather than a chance to make a difference in the local community. This presents her as a self-centred character.

   Even when the Inspector implies that Mrs Birling's actions caused Eva/Daisy to turn to suicide, she callously admits: *"I accept no blame"*. Instead, Mrs Birling tries to shift the blame onto Eva/Daisy and the father of the child. Mrs Birling's lack of sympathy towards Eva/Daisy is the clearest indication that she doesn't care about anyone but herself and her family. Mrs Birling fails to learn from the Inspector's message about social responsibility, and only seems to care when Birling believes there will be a *"public scandal"* that could damage the family's reputation.

   In conclusion, Priestley presents Mrs Birling as self-centred and resistant to his message about looking after other people in society. Mrs Birling is prejudiced against those less fortunate than herself, believing that the working class were to blame for their own poverty, rather than recognising that it was a symptom of an unfair society. Mrs Birling represents the older generation who were resistant to change because they were set in their ways, and knew that reform would weaken their position in society. By presenting Mrs Birling in this unflattering way, Priestley would have hoped that audience members would have recognised her selfishness, and would try to act with more compassion.

LEVELS-BASED MARK SCHEMES FOR EXTENDED RESPONSE QUESTIONS

Questions that require extended writing use mark bands. The whole answer will be marked together to determine which mark band it fits into and which mark should be awarded within the mark band.

The descriptors have been written in simple language to give an indication of the expectations of each mark band. See the AQA website for the official mark schemes used.

Level	Students' answers tend to...
6 (26–30 marks)	• Focus on the text as conscious construct (i.e. a play written by Priestley intended to have a deliberate effect). • Produce a logical and well-structured response which closely uses the text to explore their argument / interpretation. • Analyse the writer's craft by considering the effects of a writer's choice, linked closely to meanings. • Understand the writer's purpose and context.
5 (21–25 marks)	• Start to think about ideas in a more developed way. • Think about the deeper meaning of a text and start to explore alternative interpretations. • Start to focus on specific elements of writer's craft, linked to meanings. • Focus more on abstract concepts, such as themes and ideas, than narrative events or character feelings.
4 (16–20 marks)	• Sustain a focus on an idea, or a particular technique. • Start to consider how the text works and what the writer is doing. • Use examples effectively to support their points. • Explain the effect of a writer's method on the text, with a clear focus on it having been consciously written. • Show an understanding of ideas and themes.
3 (11–15 marks)	• Explain their ideas. • Demonstrate knowledge of the text as a whole. • Show awareness of the concept of themes. • Identify the effects of a range of methods on reader.
2 (6–10 marks)	• Support their comments by using references to / from the text. • Make comments that are generally relevant to the question. • Identify at least one method and possibly make some comment on the effect of it on the reader.
1 (1–5 marks)	• Describe the text. • Retell the narrative. • Make references to, rather than use references from, the text.
0 marks	Nothing worthy of credit / nothing written.

INDEX

A
abortion 7
Act One 14, 16–19
Act Three 24–27
Act Two 20–23
alcoholism 21, 38
allegory 13
assessment objectives vi

B
Brumley 4
Brumley Women's Charity Organisation 22

C
capitalism 14, 28, 48
class 4
   middle class 4, 6
   upper class 4, 6
   working class 5, 6
cliff hangers 10
climatic curtains 10
conversational language 12
cyclical structure 10

D
Daisy Renton 19, 21, 22, 24, 45, 46, 52
David Lloyd George 8
detective thrillers 2
dialogue 12
dramatic irony 4, 13, 14

E
Edna 46
engagement 14, 22
entrances 10
Eric 14, 18, 24–27, 38, 39, 49, 54
etiquette 7, 32
euphemisms 24
Eva Smith 15–17, 19, 24, 45, 46, 52
exits 10

F
First World War 2, 8, 14, 48
foreshadowing 13–15, 38

G
gender 51
generational differences 56, 57
Gerald 14, 15, 17–22, 26, 27, 40, 41, 49, 54

I
infidelity 7
Inspector Goole 15–17, 19–21, 25, 42, 43, 48, 53
intervals 10

J
J. B. Priestley 2, 8, 47

L
Labour Party 9, 47
Lady Croft 6, 40
Liberal Party 6

M
Milwards 18
misogynistic society 7
morality 3
morality play 2, 3, 18, 19, 21, 23
mouthpiece 42
Mr Birling 14–16, 26–30, 48, 53
Mrs Birling 14, 20– 22, 26, 27, 32–34, 48, 52

N
National Insurance 47
naturalistic theatre 11, 12
nepotism 39
NHS 9

O
omnipotence 19

P
Palace Bar 21, 24
patriarchal society 7, 51, 53
photograph 16, 17, 22, 26
Postscripts 9
prejudice 5, 17, 23, 29, 33
Priestley, J. B. 2, 8, 47

S
Second World War 8, 25, 48
seven deadly sins 3, 23
   envy 3, 19, 35
   gluttony 3, 21
   greed 3, 16
   lust 3
   pride 3, 23, 33
   wrath 3
sex work 41, 46
Sheila 14, 17–22, 26, 27, 35, 36, 49, 51
socialism 2, 6
social responsibility 2, 15, 47–49
stage directions 11
suffragettes 7

T
The Titanic 4

W
whodunnits 2
Winston Churchill 9

NOTES, DOODLES AND EXAM DATES

Doodles

Key dates

Paper 1:
....

Paper 2:
....

ACKNOWLEDGMENTS

The questions in the ClearRevise textbook are the sole responsibility of the authors and have neither been provided nor approved by the examination board.

Every effort has been made to trace and acknowledge ownership of copyright. The publishers will be happy to make any future amendments with copyright owners that it has not been possible to contact. The publisher would like to thank the following companies and individuals who granted permission for the use of their images in this textbook.

Quotes from *An Inspector Calls and Other Plays* by J. B. Priestley published by Penguin Classics. Copyright © 1947 by J. B. Priestley. Reprinted by permission of Penguin Books Limited.

Page 2 — © Pictorial Press Ltd / Alamy Stock Photo

Page 3 — © Donald Cooper / Photostage

Page 4 — *The Titanic* © Everett Collection / Shutterstock

Page 4   British group in horse drawn carriage © Vintage Images / Alamy Stock Photo

Page 5 — © Heritage Image Partnership Ltd / Alamy Stock Photo

Page 6 — © Pictorial Press Ltd / Alamy Stock Photo

Page 7 — © Pictorial Press Ltd / Alamy Stock Photo

Page 8 — Female workers in a British steel factory © Military Images / Alamy Stock Photo

Page 8 — British World War 1 soldiers © Everett Collection / Shutterstock

Page 9 — © Shawshots / Alamy Stock Photo

Page 10 — © David Jensen / Alamy Stock Photo

Page 15 — © David Jensen / Alamy Stock Photo

Page 17 — © David Jensen / Alamy Stock Photo

Page 18 — © Donald Cooper / Photostage

Page 19 — © Donald Cooper / Photostage

Page 20 — © David Jensen / Alamy Stock Photo

Page 21 — © Donald Cooper / Photostage

Page 22 — © Everett Collection Inc / Alamy Stock Photo

Page 23 — © Donald Cooper / Photostage

Page 26 — © Donald Cooper / Alamy Stock Photo

Page 27 — © Donald Cooper / Photostage

Page 28 — © Donald Cooper / Photostage

Page 29 — © Donald Cooper / Photostage

Page 30 — © Donald Cooper / Photostage

Page 32 — © David Jensen / Alamy Stock Photo

Page 34 — © Donald Cooper / Photostage

Page 35 — © Donald Cooper / Photostage

Page 38 — © Donald Cooper / Photostage

Page 39 — Donald Cooper / Photostage

Page 40 — © Donald Cooper / Photostage

Page 41 — © Donald Cooper / Photostage

Page 42 — © theatrepix / Alamy Stock Photo

Page 46 — © Donald Cooper / Photostage

Page 48 — © Everett Collection / Shutterstock

Page 51 — © Donald Cooper / Photostage

Page 52 — © thislife pictures / Alamy Stock Photo

Page 53 — © David Jensen / Alamy Stock Photo

Page 54 — © Donald Cooper / Photostage

Page 56 — © Donald Cooper / Photostage

Page 57 — © Donald Cooper / Photostage

All other photos and graphics © Shutterstock

EXAMINATION TIPS

With your examination practice, use a boundary approximation using the following table. Be aware that the grade boundaries can vary from year to year, so they should be used as a guide only.

Grade	9	8	7	6	5	4	3	2	1
Boundary	88%	79%	71%	61%	52%	43%	31%	21%	10%

1. Read the question carefully. Don't give an answer to a question that you think is appearing (or wish was appearing!) rather than the actual question.
2. Spend time reading through the question, and decide which moments from the play are the most relevant and will provide the best examples.
3. It's worth jotting down a quick plan to make sure your answer includes sufficient detail and is focused on the question.
4. Start your answer with a brief introduction where you summarise the main points of your response. This can help your answer to stay on-track.
5. A discussion of Priestley's methods can include his language choices, but also structural choices (such as the ordering of events), how characters develop, and what their actions tell you about their characterisation.
6. Include details from the text to support your answer. These details might be quotes, or they can be references to the text.
7. Make sure your handwriting is legible. The examiner can't award you marks if they can't read what you've written.
8. The examiner will be impressed if you can correctly use technical terms like 'dramatic irony', 'naturalistic theatre', 'climatic curtain', 'euphemism' etc, but to get the best marks you need to explore the effect of these techniques.
9. Use linking words and phrases to show you are developing your points or comparing information, for example, "this reinforces", "this shows that" and "on the other hand". This helps to give your answer structure, and makes it easier for the examiner to award you marks.
10. If you need extra paper, make sure you clearly signal that your answer is continued elsewhere. Remember that longer answers don't necessarily score more highly than shorter, more concise answers.
11. There are 4 marks available for spelling, punctuation and grammar. Save some time at the end of the exam to read through your answer and correct any mistakes.

Good luck!

New titles coming soon!

Revision, re-imagined

These guides are everything you need to ace your exams and beam with pride. Each topic is laid out in a beautifully illustrated format that is clear, approachable and as concise and simple as possible.

They have been expertly compiled and edited by subject specialists, highly experienced examiners, industry professionals and a good dollop of scientific research into what makes revision most effective. Past examination questions are essential to good preparation, improving understanding and confidence.

- Hundreds of marks worth of examination style questions
- Answers provided for all questions within the books
- Illustrated topics to improve memory and recall
- Specification references for every topic
- Examination tips and techniques
- Free Python solutions pack (CS Only)

Absolute clarity is the aim.

Explore the series and add to your collection at **www.clearrevise.com**

Available from all good book shops

amazon   @pgonlinepub

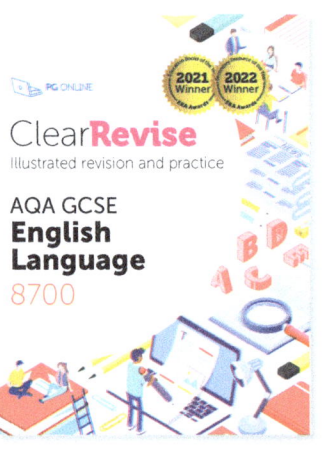

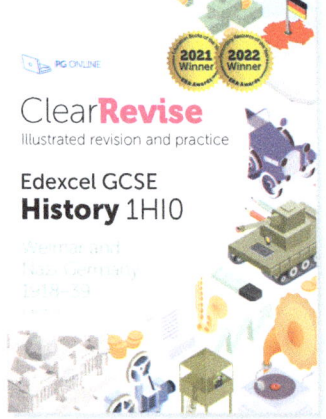

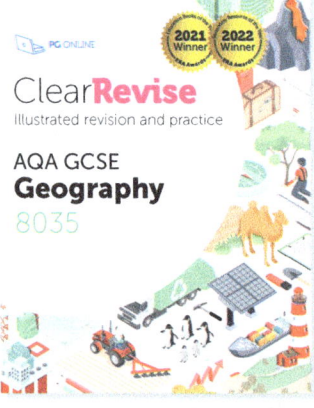

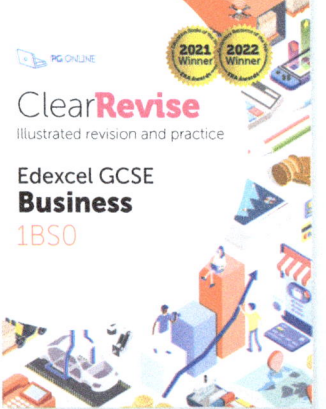

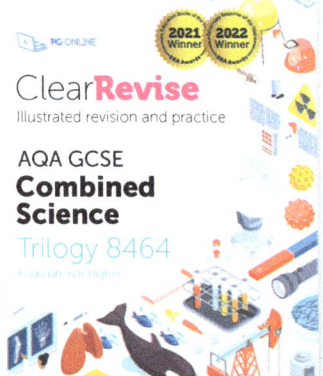

MathsPractice — Step-by-step guidance and practice
Edexcel GCSE Maths Foundation 1MA1

ClearRevise — Illustrated revision and practice
OCR Creative iMedia

ClearRevise AQA GCSE English Language 8700

ClearRevise Edexcel GCSE History 1HI0

ClearRevise AQA GCSE Geography 8035

ClearRevise OCR GCSE Computer Science J277

ClearRevise AQA GCSE English Literature Macbeth By William Shakespeare

ClearRevise Edexcel GCSE Business 1BS0

ClearRevise AQA GCSE Combined Science Trilogy 8464

ClearRevise AQA GCSE Design and Technology